AISING ATTENTION

A supportive guide for parents and carers of **children with ADHD** and **explosive behaviour**

SARAH OCKWELL-SMITH

PIATKUS

PIATKUS

First published in Great Britain in 2025 by Piatkus

1 3 5 7 9 10 8 6 4 2

Copyright © Sarah Ockwell-Smith, 2025

The moral right of the author has been asserted.

A CIP catalogue record for this book
is available from the British Library.

ISBN: 978-0-349-44430-7

Typeset in Stone Serif by M Rules
Illustrations by Liane Payne

Printed and bound in Great Britain by
Clays Ltd, Elcograf S.p.A.

Papers used by Piatkus are from well-managed forests
and other responsible sources.

MIX
Paper | Supporting
responsible forestry
FSC
www.fsc.org   FSC® C104740

Piatkus
An imprint of
Little, Brown Book Group
Carmelite House
50 Victoria Embankment
London EC4Y 0DZ

The authorised representative
in the EEA is
Hachette Ireland
8 Castlecourt Centre, Dublin 15,
D15 XTP3, Ireland
(email: info@hbgi.ie)

An Hachette UK Company

www.hachette.co.uk
www.littlebrown.co.uk

The information given in this book is not intended to replace any
advice given by a health professional. If you have any concerns about
your child's health, physical or mental, contact the appropriate health
professional. The author and publisher disclaim any liability directly or
indirectly from the use of the information in this book by any person.

Contents

Introduction

The path of a parent who has a child displaying explosive behaviour can be a lonely one. I want to start this book by telling
you that you are not alone, especially on the days when you feel
isolated and ostracised. If I could reach through this page and
give you a hug, I would, because I know you probably need it.

You may know me as a 'parenting expert' – a gentle-parenting
guru who is all about staying calm and being a great role model –
and perhaps you believe I possess some sort of natural ability
to know all the answers. I want to tell you that, like much of
parenting witnessed online, this is an illusion. Underneath the
surface and the calm persona, I've been hiding a secret: that is
quite how much I have struggled over the last two decades.

I have been at rock bottom as a parent, and I've dug a multi-
level basement beneath that, too. There have been days (many
of them, if I'm honest) when I've questioned why anybody
would listen to my advice. There have been days when other
professionals have insinuated that I am a bad parent and school
leadership have told me that *I* am 'the problem' (much more
later on the gaslighting many of us, including you, I suspect,
experience as the parents of an explosive or neurodivergent
child). There have also been days when I honestly didn't feel
like I could go on anymore. I kept this information private for
several reasons. First, out of respect for my child (who is now
an adult and happy to share our story in this book); second,

because it was too painful and raw to talk about (I now feel in a place where I'm able to share); and third, well, you can't be a 'parenting expert' if you admit quite how much you struggle as a parent yourself, can you?

Why am I writing this book now? you may ask. Because I've realised that embracing and accepting your own flaws and talking about your difficult days is so important as a parent. I feel far enough along my own family's journey now for it not to be painful to talk about it anymore, my son, as I said, is old enough to give his full consent for me to talk about his struggles and I genuinely feel I have insights and wisdom to share that will help you. I also feel that this book is desperately needed. When I was searching for information about how to parent through the maze of attention deficit hyperactivity disorder (ADHD) and explosive behaviour, all I found was outdated, behaviourist, authoritarian advice that made my heart sore and my child feel (and behave) significantly worse. The parenting courses that several professionals tried to make me take were similar.

We need a revolution in the way society speaks about ADHD and difficult behaviour in childhood, and we need to drastically change the way we treat the individuals involved, both parents and children. For the last couple of years, I have felt a calling to contribute to that revolution. This book is my contribution to the cause. It is also the encouragement, the virtual hug and the non-judgemental listening ear I wish I had found when I was at my lowest point. I hope to be able to lift you out of yours a little.

Who is this book for?

In short, this book is for any adult who cares for a child with explosive behaviour, whether they have a diagnosis of ADHD or not. You will find lots of information here about ADHD, but it applies equally to those who may have a different diagnosis, are early in the diagnostic pathway or have no diagnosis at all. On that note, please forgive me if I occasionally just refer to ADHD and not explosive behaviour – the information I discuss will apply equally to any of the scenarios just mentioned.

This book is for adults who care for children who struggle to regulate their behaviour, who are prone to outbreaks of violence (including, but not limited to: hitting, kicking, slapping, biting, throwing, pushing, banging and smashing), who act impulsively, don't listen to instructions, frequently break the rules, show deliberate defiance and destructive behaviour (including verbally). It doesn't matter if the child is your own, one you look after or one you teach, although you will find specific help for those who are struggling with parenting.

This is a book for adults who care about children, who want to understand them and behaviour that is so often described as 'naughty'. It is a book for adults who want to help children and who are willing to make changes to their own behaviour and beliefs in order to do so. Ultimately, this book is a love letter to children with ADHD and those who struggle with their behaviour – and for the adults in their lives who care about them.

A QUICK NOTE ON TERMINOLOGY

Throughout this book, I will use the terms neurotypical and neurodivergent. In case you haven't come across them before, I wanted to quickly explain them:

Neurotypical This word is used to describe individuals whose brains develop as expected, according to standard neurophysiology. They will learn, behave and perceive the world in a way that is expected according to societal norms.

Neurodivergent This word is used to describe individuals whose brains are wired differently to the ones of those who are neurotypical, and whose behaviour deviates from the social norm, alongside having different ways to learn and understand the world.

What is this book about?

Let me start with what it's *not* about.

You won't find lengthy and detailed descriptions of how to get an ADHD diagnosis, how to get an Education, Health and Care Plan (EHCP) in place, or how to understand the legalities of disability discrimination. I have deliberately not included these for four reasons:

First, I don't want to reinvent the wheel. There are many amazing charities and organisations who offer support and advice on these issues. Instead of repeating this information, I have instead signposted to them in the Resources section (see page 223). Second, I am acutely aware that while I am based in England, UK, not all of my readers are, and rather than give you very English-centric advice, my aim is to provide information that will help no matter where you live in the world (though you will find some country-specific Resources on page 223. Third, I'm hoping for something of a reform in the way our society approaches neurodivergence and SEND (special educational needs and disabilities), and so I hope that any information I could include about diagnostic pathways or educational support will quickly become out of date (perhaps wishful thinking, but I'm keeping my fingers crossed!). And fourth, my intention with this book is to provide a sort of manual to support you in caring for and raising children with big, explosive behaviours. I don't want to take away from the core idea with detours into medical pathways, educational policy and different legal systems; my focus is on increasing awareness and understanding of why some children act in the way they do and what adults can do to help them.

When I was in your position, what I really wanted was to feel heard and supported and for somebody who had been in my situation to give me advice on how to help my child, alongside some tips on how I could cope better, so that's exactly what this book will focus on, without the noise of anything else.

Now, what *will* you find in this book?

Let me walk you through some of the main content you'll find in each chapter.

We start the book with an exploration of ADHD and explosive behaviour in Chapter One, posing the questions of how you know if your child has ADHD and when – if ever – you should seek a diagnosis. While this chapter is initially aimed at those who do not yet have a diagnosis for their child, we soon include those of you who are a little further along the path, with a child who is already diagnosed with ADHD. In this chapter we also consider other conditions that often co-exist with ADHD, such as autism, sensory processing disorder (SPD) and pathological demand avoidance (PDA), and yet are so often missed in the initial diagnosis. Although Chapter One talks about diagnoses, I am firmly of the opinion that all children should be treated as individuals, with unique needs, rather than medicalising, stereo-typing and labelling them as a whole – a point we will explore more in this chapter and, indeed, throughout the whole book.

Chapter Two covers the many myths and misunderstandings surrounding children with ADHD and explosive behaviour; from screentime to vaccines, ultra-processed diets to a lack of play and the new kid on the block: childhood trauma. Almost everybody seems to have an opinion about the cause of ADHD and how overdiagnosed it is today. This chapter aims to sort the wheat from the chaff, the evidence and the realities of ADHD. I'll also give you some tips on how to handle people who constantly offer you unsolicited advice and ridiculous opinions.

Chapter Three is titled 'It's not their fault'. I believe that removing the blame that is so often heaped on children is key when attempting to help them to regulate their behaviour. Too many children are labelled 'naughty' and punished, chastised, lectured and cajoled into trying to change their behaviour to please adults. When they inevitably fall short of the desired behaviour, they find themselves in a vicious circle of failure, punishment, disappointment and dented self-esteem. The most important concept for parents and carers of children with explosive behaviour to understand is that as much as they wish their children could behave 'better', I'm pretty sure the children wish it more. In this chapter, we will explore some of the underlying reasons for some of the difficult behaviour you are probably so used to seeing, and why blaming children is not only ineffective, but potentially makes things a whole lot worse.

Chapter Four is all about getting to the root of your child's explosive behaviour, identifying their triggers and working with them to try to prevent meltdowns and eruptions. Of course, this isn't always possible, and so Chapter Five is all about how to cope when your child's behaviour is out of control and what to do in the moments when you yourself feel out of control, too. It also looks at concerns for other children you may have (especially if they are neurotypical). These two chapters contain the practical tips and nitty gritty of how to work with your child's behaviour; however, please don't be tempted to skip the earlier chapters and focus solely on these – they will make much more sense having read Chapters One to Three first.

In Chapter Six we turn our attention to education, or, specifically, how to help your child survive (and preferably thrive) at school when they have lots of big, difficult behaviour. We discuss navigating school-behaviour systems, relationships with school staff and how they can help your child. We also talk about school avoidance and alternatives to mainstream education that may be better suited to your child. It isn't only daytime behaviour that parents and carers of children with ADHD and undiagnosed explosive behaviour struggle with – behaviour at night is often tricky, too. Sleep struggles are common among neurodivergent children, and so the whole of Chapter Seven is devoted to these, covering everything from bedtime refusal, difficulties falling asleep to problems staying asleep, and many ways in which you can help to improve your child's sleep (and maybe your own, too).

The last three chapters of the book turn the focus from children to ourselves: the adults. In Chapter Eight we consider the possibility that it isn't just our children who may have a diagnosable condition. Indeed, there are strong hereditary links when it comes to neurodivergence (something we discuss in Chapters One and Three), and it is highly likely that you yourself, or other members of your child's close family, have a condition that perhaps you're not aware of, despite having always felt a little different. I've called this chapter 'Unmasking Ourselves' because often it is only when a child is diagnosed that a parent realises there is a reason for so many of the things they themselves have experienced in life and finally discover their authentic self.

Chapter Nine picks up on the idea that, contrary to societal opinion, a child's difficult behaviour is rarely the fault of parents. Parents of children with ADHD and undiagnosed explosive behaviour almost always find themselves in a sinkhole of blame and guilt. Was it something you did? Something you didn't do? Something you didn't do well enough? Is it your fault? Are you a bad parent? I can tell you right now that you're not, and it's not your fault. In Chapter Nine we'll explore this in much more detail and hopefully reach a point where you finally stop blaming yourself.

Finally, Chapter Ten is again all about you. In this final chapter, we discuss the common feelings experienced by parents of children with ADHD and explosive behaviour, from despair and exhaustion, to guilt, shame and embarrassment. One of the key messages in this book that you will read time and time again is the idea that we need to accept our children as they are, rather than trying to change them. We can't change our children, but we can try to change our own thoughts and behaviours. This chapter, I hope, will help you to do just that. There is no added guilt or pressure from me (I'm sure you pile enough of both on yourself already), just empathy and support.

What age children does this book apply to?

Any. It doesn't matter if you have a four-year-old, a fourteen-year-old or even a twenty-year-old. This book is about understanding your child, at their current level of development, and working with them to improve their behaviour alongside improving your knowledge and confidence as their parent. Age is irrelevant.

What qualifies me to write this book?

I was asked this question by somebody on social media when I announced I was writing this book and it has really stayed with me. I have pretty terrible imposter syndrome (more on this in Chapter Eight) and I have resisted writing this book for many years, not just in order to protect my son and because I was still processing everything we have been through, but also because I kept asking myself if I could do it justice. After ruminating on this for far longer than necessary, I've come to the conclusion that I think I can. I have lived this journey for over two decades now. There is not much research I haven't read or hurdles we haven't had to jump as a family. You'll hear a lot about our experiences and thoughts throughout the chapters of this book. If you've read any of my other books, prepare for far more personal information than I've ever shared before.

I have always said I would only write about a topic that I have personal experience of, and I have experience of raising a child with ADHD in spades. That said, I am also very aware of the feelings of the neurodivergent community and particularly the idea of writing 'nothing about us without us'. To this end, I am indebted to the many children and adults with ADHD who have contributed their stories to this book. To really understand, and to be the best parents and carers we can possibly be to a child with ADHD or undiagnosed explosive behaviour, we have to listen to them and their lived experience.

I'd like to close this Introduction with some words from my son, Flynn (age twenty-one at the time of publication). Flynn was finally diagnosed with ADHD when he was fourteen, eight long years after I first raised my suspicions with professionals:

> *I think you have to accept the child, rather than trying to change them. Understanding and patience is the best way to help.*

Chapter One

Exploring explosive behaviour and ADHD

While planning this book, I grappled with what to include in the opening chapter. The logical place to start is with an explanation of explosive behaviour and considering if it may be undiagnosed ADHD. For those whose children are currently undiagnosed, I suspect you may be seeking guidance to aid you with receiving a diagnosis and, ultimately, using that to inform your parenting. For those whose children have already received a diagnosis, I suspect the expectation when choosing this book may be that it contains instructions for how best to discipline a child with ADHD.

Children with ADHD are not a homogeneous blob. They do not all need the same thing. What each of them needs from their parents and caregivers is entirely unique. The ADHD label should not override this. The approach I feel most comfortable with, therefore, is helping you to understand your wonderfully unique child and to learn how best to meet their needs (and your own). A metaphor I like to use often when I speak with parents is about caring for plants. I'm an avid gardener and quickly learned that the soil, feed and care that I give to my hydrangeas so that they can thrive is not the same that I would give to my lilacs. They are both perennial flowering shrubs, but their needs are very different. The same is true of children with ADHD. Your child is as unique the day after they receive a diagnosis as they were the day before. What works for some parents raising children with ADHD will not work for you and your child. We must see the individual first, always.

This book is not written through a diagnostic lens; it is written through an inclusive one, that centres your child, their needs, their feelings and their experiences. As we move through the chapters, you will find that the advice within them is equally applicable to children who have an ADHD diagnosis and those who do not. For many years now, parents have been asking me to write 'a gentle-parenting book for children with ADHD'. I have often resisted these calls, because to me, gentle parenting works for all children – the beauty of it is that it is not a 'one-size-fits-all' approach, but a flexible one. Nothing changes if they have a diagnosis. That said, over the years, I have come to understand that parenting advice for children with ADHD is often the complete opposite of gentle parenting, with talk of strict discipline and consequences. If I'm honest, most of the advice I give in this book applies to all children, including those who are neurotypical; however, I do feel parents of children with ADHD, or undiagnosed explosive behaviour, need extra guidance with how best to apply gentle parenting.

What is gentle parenting?

Over the last decade, the awareness of gentle parenting practices has exploded, attracting constant media attention. Unfortunately, as its popularity has soared, so have the myths and the misconceptions. In fact, I barely recognise the gentle parenting discussed on social media or in sensationalised media reports today. For me, it is something far simpler. In *The Gentle Parenting Book*, published in 2016, I defined gentle parenting as having four cornerstones: understanding, empathy, respect and boundaries. That's understanding the neurological and physical capabilities of children and setting our expectations of them in a way that is realistic and achievable; empathy for what children are experiencing and considering their thoughts and feelings as well as our own; adults respecting children as standard, rather than demanding that they blindly respect us; and, finally, a focus on the all-important boundaries, which are used to teach, guide and keep children safe.

Gentle parenting, in my opinion, is the only effective way to raise children with ADHD and explosive behaviour, because it's the only style that is truly informed about their neurodivergence, their experiences of their world, their emotions and motivations and the stigma and stereotypes they face on a daily basis. All children should be treated with respect, but those with difficult behaviour are in desperate need of it, instead of the harsh, controlling parenting they are often at the receiving end of. Children with ADHD do not need special parenting, or even a special version of gentle parenting; they just need gentle parenting applied in a way that takes into account their brain development, neurological capabilities and emotion processing. This book is effectively my guide to gentle parenting for children with ADHD and explosive behaviour. I may not refer to gentle parenting much throughout the book, but the ethos underpins all the advice in it.

What do I mean by explosive behaviour?

All children struggle with their behaviour. Or perhaps I should say all parents and carers struggle with the behaviour of children. We expect far too much of them, often wanting them to behave better than we do ourselves. We expect them to sit still, be quiet, do what is asked of them, sleep when we want them to, eat when we want them to and speak when we want them to (and not when we don't). We expect them to be able to regulate their emotions, suppressing anger, frustration and disappointment at will in order to appease social and moral rules. We expect them to acquiesce and follow our instructions, even if they are unhappy with them. Life is pretty tough for a child.

Understandably, children often struggle to follow the guidelines to 'be good' and tantrums are common (long after toddlerhood). Some children seem to struggle more than others, though. These are the children who are frequently angry and often violent, despite their parents' and carers' best efforts to calm them. The parents and carers of these children will often message me and ask for my advice saying, 'I've tried all the gentle-parenting stuff and none of it works. I am at my wits' end. I hate saying it, but my child is completely out of control, and I don't know what to do any more.'

Children with explosive behaviour will often lash out physically, throwing, hitting, pushing, shoving, biting and slapping long after their peers have outgrown this sort of behaviour. They shout, swear, curse and answer back. They will often find themselves on the receiving end of detentions, isolations, suspensions and sometimes expulsions at school. Sometimes – often, in fact – they can be wonderful and kind and loving. Then, just like that, they will snap and explode with rage, sometimes verbal, sometimes physical.

Raising an explosive child often feels impossible. It is confusing, scary, heart-wrenching and exhausting. Perhaps you can relate to something I have written here? If so, this book is for you.

Do all children with explosive behaviour have ADHD?

In short, no. In fact, I find that many in gentle-parenting circles rush to suggest that children have ADHD if their behaviour is explosive, or deemed 'out of control', and this isn't always the case. What is true, though, is that these children are struggling with something, and the key to gentle parenting is to find out what. As I said at the beginning of this chapter, children with ADHD are not a homogeneous blob and neither are children with explosive behaviour. What all children with explosive behaviour need, however, are caregivers who are kind, curious and supportive. They don't all need a diagnosis of ADHD.

Do children with ADHD always have explosive behaviour?

Absolutely not! Some children have a type of ADHD where the dysregulation and hyperactivity so often associated with it are internal, without any externalised difficult behaviours (more on this in a minute). That said, just because you can't see the evidence of their dysregulation, it doesn't mean they aren't experiencing any. Some children with ADHD are prone to what I call imploding behaviour, in that they often turn their frustrations inwards and become both the source and casualty of their thoughts. This type of internalised dysregulation can manifest as anxiety, anger, frustration, depression, self-deprecating thoughts, self-hatred and self-condemnation. Some children, particularly girls, are good at masking these feelings and parents can often be surprised at how much they have been struggling, especially as they seem so 'good' when it comes to their external behaviour. Again, much more on this later.

How do you know if your child has ADHD?

This is the million-dollar question. I wish I had an easy, step-by-step answer for you – a sort of ADHD flow chart, if you like. I'm afraid I don't, though. My best answer is to trust your gut instinct. Do you have a feeling that your child is different from their peers? Or even their siblings (if their siblings are neuro-typical, that is)? Is the idea on your mind a lot and you've not managed to convince yourself otherwise? Do you find yourself googling 'symptoms of ADHD in children' late at night? Or joining social media groups for parents of neurodivergent children to ascertain if their children are similar to yours? Has your childminder, nursery or preschool keyworker or schoolteacher raised it as a possibility with you? If you can answer 'yes' to any of these, then I think there is a definite possibility. Physicians are trained to trust parental instinct when a parent brings a child into the accident and emergency department; I think the same should be true of ADHD. If you feel, deep in your heart, that your child may have ADHD, then trust those niggles – they are rarely wrong.

Should you get your child diagnosed?

I have to start by challenging this terminology. Should you *get* your child diagnosed? The 'get' implies that the child is passive and the parent has full control. 'Get' implies that any diagnosis is something that is done *to* the child, regardless of whether they give consent or not, because the parent wants a diagnosis. The first question we should actually be asking is: 'What does my child want?' Working collaboratively with your child, listening to their feelings and actually taking them on board has to be your starting point. Of course, in order for your child to give their consent to pursuing a diagnosis, they have to understand not only the process, but also any potential negative repercussions, as well as positive outcomes that may stem from it. If you find yourself instinctively feeling that your child has a differently wired brain and that pursuing a diagnosis is something that would benefit your family, do make sure that your child is keen and ready to explore it before you book any appointments.

Weighing up the pros and cons of diagnosis

There can, undoubtedly, be a social stigma surrounding an ADHD diagnosis. On the one hand, your child receiving a diagnosis may help to reduce negative comments and treatment concerning their behaviour; on the other, many people still have issues surrounding 'labelling children' and these negative views may increase once people find out your child's diagnosis.

I don't think there is any straightforward answer regarding seeking a diagnosis. Once again, I think it comes back to trusting your gut and your child. If you are a pros-and-cons-type person, you may find the following table helpful. Perhaps you could jot down a few of your own thoughts, and those of your child, too, if you are still undecided.

Pros of diagnosis	Cons of diagnosis
Others may be kinder to the child once they know the underlying cause of their behaviour.	Concerns that others will treat your child poorly because of the diagnosis and their own opinions of ADHD.

Pros of diagnosis

A diagnosis may provide validation, for both parent and child, helping to alleviate some parental guilt. This validation may help them to be a better parent and also aid them in developing a deeper understanding of their child's needs.

As the child gets older, they can learn more about ADHD and understand their own thoughts and behaviours more, which can help with their self-esteem and self-confidence.

A diagnosis opens up access to medication if this is desired by the child and their family.

ADHD can be considered a disability (as per the Equality Act 2010 in the UK) and therefore a diagnosis can give legal protection against unfair treatment, especially in education settings and later in the workplace.

A diagnosis can bring extra support and understanding for children who attend school and further- and higher-education institutions. In some countries they may also be entitled to financial support.

Cons of diagnosis

Some people believe that the current DSM-V (Diagnostic and Statistical Manual of Mental Disorders – version 5) definition used for a diagnosis is unreliable and problematic. There are no clinical tests for ADHD, therefore a diagnosis is based upon an assessment of externalised behaviours, not a measurable internal pathology, which can leave space for misdiagnosis.

Some believe that a diagnosis may result in a sort of self-fulfilling prophecy, with all poor behaviour blamed on ADHD, which may unconsciously bias the future of the growing child.

Some families are not keen on the idea of medication and feel they are pushed towards it once their child receives a diagnosis.

Framing ADHD as a disability (and therefore viewing the child as disabled) can be seen as derogatory by some. Others believe that a medical diagnosis of a 'disorder' pathologises the child unnecessarily and may be harmful to their self-esteem.

Many schools are unable to support children with ADHD, despite their diagnosis, due to insufficient funding, and some teachers may have an unconscious bias concerning expected behaviour of children with ADHD.

Another important point to consider is that once a child is diagnosed, there is a tendency for parents and carers to treat them in ways that are considered 'good for ADHD'. This approach completely misses the child's individuality and distinct needs. As we discussed at the beginning of this chapter, children with ADHD are not a homogeneous blob and they don't all need the same things, however much parenting and discipline advice might suggest otherwise. There is a danger that a diagnosis can pigeonhole a child and create self-fulfilling prophecies when it comes to behaviour and expectations. Regardless of whether your child receives a diagnosis or not, accepting them as a wonderfully unique being with unique needs is perhaps the best advice I could give you.

One of the top arguments I hear regarding pursuing a diagnosis is that they unnecessarily label children. But if your child has a label of ADHD, this is arguably better than any label society may try to pin on them (such as 'naughty', 'poorly behaved' or 'difficult') and significantly better than any they may assign to themselves (such as 'useless', 'stupid' and 'a failure'). The label of ADHD should not be one of stigma; it should be one of understanding, validation and support, and so it is one I personally was happy to embrace, especially given the alternatives.

I always suggest thinking, *What's the worst that will happen if a child is diagnosed with ADHD?* They are likely already stigmatised because of their behaviour; parents are usually at their wits' end and desperate for help. Starting from a position of rock bottom, as my family did, generally means things can only get better post-diagnosis, with more understanding and validation. I hope that one day we can move on from fears of pathologising children and labelling them to viewing a diagnosis as a way to support them.

WHEN IS THE RIGHT TIME TO PURSUE A DIAGNOSIS?

While children can receive an ADHD diagnosis as young as three years of age, most health professionals prefer to wait until they are four and over. Partly, this is due to most children starting school at four or five years of age, which means being able to observe their behaviour in two different settings (at home and at school). The other concern with seeking a diagnosis for a toddler or preschooler is that explosive, out-of-control behaviour is common at this age and there is a fine line between what is considered 'normal' behaviour in very young children and what may be a symptom of ADHD. Some children may be much older when they are diagnosed and, as I've already touched upon, many don't receive a diagnosis until adulthood.

As to the 'right time', I don't think there is one. I knew that my son was different to his siblings from late toddlerhood, but I wasn't certain that he had ADHD until he was around six or seven years old. From experience, I would say forget waiting until a specific age – your parental instinct is so much more powerful than statistics. The right time to pursue a diagnosis is when you feel that one will benefit your child and your family and when your child (if they are old enough to discuss and understand) is happy to pursue one.

Is it right to call ADHD a disorder?

A major stumbling block concerning seeking and receiving an ADHD diagnosis is in the name itself: attention deficit hyperactivity *disorder*. Using the word 'disorder' is viewed by many as insulting. It implies there is something wrong with the child, that they are not 'normal', that they are somehow broken, or flawed. While their brains are differently wired and this often causes them to struggle, the idea that their difficulties are a pathological problem is one that does not sit well with many neurodivergent people. For some parents, the suggestion that their child has a disorder does not sit well with them either and they may avoid a diagnosis for this reason.

If we look at the neurobiology of the brain of an individual with ADHD, there are differences that deviate from the norm. The brain of a child with ADHD develops in a way that is considered abnormal. Therefore, medically speaking, the word 'disorder' is appropriate. However, when we consider the whole child, rather than a medical diagnosis, it feels an uncomfortable word to use and I can understand why many dislike it. Perhaps renaming it attention deficit hyperactivity difference would be more appropriate?

Would you feel more comfortable using the word difference instead of disorder? Would your child?

Is it ADHD or ADD?

While we're on the topic of terminology, this feels like a good point at which to consider the distinction between the terms ADHD and ADD (attention deficit disorder). Many believe that ADD is the best for referring to children who do not display hyperactive behaviour. However, it is an outdated term, which has not been used medically since the 1980s.

While some children (and, indeed, adults) with ADHD do not display hyperactivity or impulsiveness, this doesn't mean that they are not experiencing it. Many describe internal mental processes of whirring thoughts and buzzing brains as a type of hyperactivity. The term ADHD is now, therefore, used in all cases, regardless of the predominant symptoms.

ADHD is commonly divided into three distinct subtypes:

Inattentive type

This type is associated with difficulties with attention and organisation, including lack of focus, difficulty following instructions and troubles with working memory. Often this type is described as 'daydreaming'; it accounts for around 20–30 per cent of all ADHD diagnoses and is the most common one seen in girls.

Hyperactive–impulsive type

This type usually shows as lots of movement, fidgeting, squirming, talking and other noisemaking, alongside lack of impulse control and making poor decisions behaviour-wise. The hyperactive–impulsive type is most commonly diagnosed in boys, and it is the one most people think about when they consider ADHD. It accounts for around 15 per cent of all ADHD diagnoses.

Combined type

The combined type of ADHD features a mix of both the inattentive and hyperactive–impulsive ones. It accounts for between 50 and 75 per cent of all ADHD diagnoses.[1]

ADHD in girls – a different presentation

If you ask most people to describe ADHD symptoms, they will often talk about the behaviour of boys they know. Girls, however, tend to present differently. That's not to say that girls do not experience hyperactive–impulsive types of ADHD or combined types – they do. However, far more experience an inattentive type. And because the symptoms of the inattentive type are not easily observed, girls who are struggling with ADHD can often be missed. It is no coincidence that the rates of diagnosis are significantly higher in boys; girls are diagnosed at less than half the rate of boys, even though ADHD is not a sex-based condition. In other words, just as many girls as boys have ADHD, but half of them fly under the radar and never receive a diagnosis, or (as we will discuss in our next chapter), they finally receive a diagnosis in adulthood.[2]

Some of this is undoubtedly due to sex-based biases and the outdated idea that ADHD is a 'boy issue', meaning that professionals working with children and their families are less likely to pick up on ADHD if the child is female. And parents themselves may miss ADHD in their daughters if they believe children with ADHD always have explosive and hyperactive behaviour.

What can ADHD look like in girls?

- Anxiety
- Daydreaming
- Disorganisation
- Easily distracted
- Emotional dysregulation
- A low tolerance to stress
- Forgetfulness
- Friendship difficulties
- Hyper-focus on things
- Messiness
- People-pleasing behaviour
- Perfectionism
- Poor self-esteem
- Procrastination
- Being sensitive to criticism
- Being socially withdrawn

- Spacing out during conversations
- Time-management difficulties

Of course, this list isn't exhaustive. It just highlights some of the traits that are common in girls and don't immediately come to mind when you think about ADHD. Some girls will also have the combined type and may exhibit some hyperactive or impulsive behaviour occasionally but they tend to be more inattentive overall. If you have a daughter who ticks many of these boxes, or perhaps you do yourself, then do consider ADHD. Our society has much work still to be done when it comes to raising awareness of ADHD symptoms in girls and women, and far too many miss out on a diagnosis and the validation and support that can come with it.

Our journey to diagnosis

I thought it may help a little if I shared my family's story of our diagnostic journey. As I mentioned earlier in this chapter, I had a strong intuition that Flynn was different to his siblings and his peers when he was very young. I vividly remember having to leave several parent-and-toddler groups early because of his behaviour and the way other parents used to stare and tut at us and move to the other side of the room if we went near to them. By the time he had started at preschool, I was certain that he was struggling with something, but I didn't know what. When he was six, I raised my concerns with the school SENCo (special educational needs co-ordinator); however, she reassured me that she didn't think he showed signs of any neurodivergence and our meeting ended with me feeling that I had overreacted.

Several incidents happened at school (one of which I'll tell you about in Chapter Ten) and I was called in to speak to his class teacher or headteacher at least once a month, often more.

Alongside this, I had become 'that mum' at the school gate, who other parents looked at and whispered about to their friends. I wish I could tell you that I was being paranoid, but I knew they were talking about Flynn and his behaviour, because often, their whispers were clearly audible, whether accidentally or perhaps on purpose. He was also never invited on playdates with their children or to their birthday parties, and when I invited them to his, they never turned up, made excuses or usually flat-out ignored the invitation. I raised my concerns with the school again. The SENCo was similarly dismissive, but this time agreed to seek advice from an educational psychologist who would observe Flynn at school.

I had no idea that the educational psychologist had visited the school to observe Flynn until he came home and said, 'Mum, some man was in my classroom today watching me.' Apparently, he did not speak with Flynn at all, just watched him for a bit. I did not have a chance to speak with the psychologist and was told I needed to wait for his report. A week or so later, I received a letter in the post. The letter was short, not even filling one sheet of paper. It ended with this statement: 'Flynn does not show signs of ADHD, he just seems to be immature for his age.' I took this personally; it felt like an attack on my parenting, as well as my child. I had overreacted again. There was nothing wrong with my son. The problem must be me. I didn't seek any further professional input for another six years.

When Flynn moved to secondary school his behaviour become more erratic and the gulf between him and his peers widened. Phone calls home became an almost daily occurrence and I was often summoned to the school to discuss his latest misdemeanours. Most of the behaviour was 'silly', rather than harmful or hurtful. He would move around a lot, say stupid things, talk back to the teachers, refuse to get started on his work in class and constantly forget books and equipment and homework. In his own words, he would 'do first, think second'.

At home, his tantrums and explosive behaviour intensified. After difficult days at school, with his self-esteem at rock bottom, he would come home and take his anger and frustration out on his father, myself and his siblings. The difficulties weren't just confined to term-time, though. The summer holidays would be extra difficult. I would sit for hours talking to him about how he should try harder, but nothing changed.

After yet another meeting with the school SENCo and deputy head, where they outright blamed my lax parenting (or in their words 'too-gentle' discipline) for Flynn's behaviour, I had an epiphany. I asked myself what I would do if I was consulting with another parent. I realised I would tell them to trust their instinct and push for the support that they so clearly needed. My instinct that Flynn was different had never gone away. I had just silenced it because so many professionals had told me it was wrong. The next morning, I called our doctor's surgery and asked for an appointment with the GP who I felt was the most supportive. He listened and agreed to refer us to a specialist paediatrician at our local Child Development Centre.

After a long wait and a lot of form filling and questionnaire completion, the big day arrived. Our hour-long appointment felt like the first time anybody had properly listened to me and taken my concerns seriously. Importantly, it was the first time a profes-sional had properly listened to Flynn. We were both in tears as he told the paediatrician of the struggles he faced on a daily basis. At the end of the appointment, we had a diagnosis – combined-type ADHD. I felt vindicated. It felt like a huge weight was lifted from us that day. Flynn received a new label, but he also lost those that he had carried for so long – 'naughty', 'disruptive', 'difficult', 'rude', 'disrespectful', 'defiant', 'badly behaved', 'immature'. We would take those four little letters any day, over all the other things he had been called for the first fourteen years of his life.

Getting a diagnosis didn't change who Flynn was, but it changed how everybody else saw him. It changed some (sadly not all) of the mistreatment he had received because of his ADHD and, most importantly, it changed how my family understood him. From that day on, we could begin to rebuild his shattered self-esteem and work to stop some of the discrimination he had faced every day. I wouldn't hesitate to seek a diagnosis again and only wish I had pushed harder earlier.

I asked Flynn what his advice would be to parents who are considering whether or not to get a diagnosis for their child. Here's what he told me:

> *My advice to any parent with a child with potential ADHD is to get them a diagnosis. My life did a full one hundred and eighty degrees after my diagnosis. Getting diagnosed meant I was able to have medication which really helped me to focus. I also felt protected by the diagnosis, as I wasn't just labelled as a naughty child anymore. I felt more seen and more heard. It helped my self-esteem to understand why I was like I was. I made more friends as they understood, and it made school easier and less of chore.*

To medicate or not medicate?

The natural next step that follows on from an ADHD diagnosis for many children is the medication discussion. There is tremendous stigma in our society concerning ADHD medication and the mistaken belief that it turns children into 'zombies'. Because of these and similar views, many parents are reluctant to consider medication for their children – sometimes through fear, sometimes because they would prefer to go down a natural route, or because of things they have read or heard about bad experiences with it.

Medication was life-changing for Flynn for the years he

chose to take it as a teenager. Now, as an adult, he has chosen to stop taking it as he feels the benefits are now outweighed by the side effects, a ratio which has certainly changed over the years for him. My aim with this section is not to persuade you to medicate your child, but rather to help you understand the medication (not the societal myths surrounding it) and enable you to at least consider it – and, if your child is old enough, for you to have a conversation with them, so that they (because, ultimately, it should be their decision, not yours) can make an informed decision about whether to take it or not.

What are they and how do they work?

Medications prescribed for ADHD fall into two distinct categories: stimulants and non-stimulants. Stimulants fall into one of two groups – methylphenidate or amphetamine – and are usually the first line of treatment for children. Methylphenidate is the most commonly prescribed medication and comes with many different brand names, including Concerta, Equasym and Ritalin.

While it may seem strange to prescribe a child with hyper-activity (either externalised or internalised) with a stimulant, the medication works to stimulate specific areas of the brain that are *under*active in children with ADHD. These areas are those that help to control attention and impulse control. For a neurotypical person, this medication may make them hyperactive, or 'high', but for a person with ADHD, they have the opposite effect. Specifically, it works to change the way dopamine is taken up by the brain, resulting in higher levels of it between brain cells. The result is that children are better able to focus and regulate their behaviour. The stimulants have a calming effect, although this is more akin to turning down the volume of their brain and taking several meditative deep breaths than the zombie-like effect that many refer to when attacking ADHD medication.

When a child is first started on medication, they will begin on a low dose and, with careful supervision, this will be titrated up (increased), until a point is reached where it is well tolerated, with as few side effects as possible and there is maximum clinical benefit.

What are the side effects?

Common side effects of methylphenidate include a dry mouth, loss of appetite (which may also result in weight loss), headaches, nausea and trouble sleeping.[3] These side effects are the reason why dosages are started low and monitored closely. Rarer side effects can include palpitations (an irregular heartbeat) and changes in blood pressure. Again, these are carefully monitored with regular physical checks. From a long-term safety perspective, these medications have been used for many decades and are considered mostly safe in the long term.[4] There is some data to suggest that the stature of a child taking ADHD medication may be shorter than it might have been without the medication, but this has not been found in all studies, and also an indication that long-term usage may impact on heart health in rare cases.

What are the positive effects?

Aside from personal accounts from children and adults, describing the positive impact of ADHD medication for them, there are some interesting studies, too. One indicates that taking medication reduces the risk of early death for people with ADHD.[5] Here, it is not the actual medication increasing an individual's lifespan, but the impact it has on reducing risky behaviours. The study found a significant reduced risk of death from unnatural causes (for example, accidents, suicide and drug overdose) when on medication. Previous research has found that those with ADHD have a higher risk of death from unnatural causes than those without it, so medication that can reduce this risk is quite literally lifesaving.[6]

When it comes to the impact on mental health, research looking at children aged between six and eighteen who were taking ADHD medication found they were significantly less likely to experience depression and anxiety than their peers who were not taking medication.[7] Finally, while many worry that medicating children may act as a gateway to illegal drugs as the child reaches their teens and adulthood, research shows quite the opposite.[8] Children are significantly less likely to engage in substance abuse in the future if they have been medicated for ADHD in childhood.

While you could read all the statistics and research papers in the world regarding medication, the most important thing to consider is what your child wants. After all, they will be the ones taking it (or not). So it needs to be their decision, with informed guidance from you and their healthcare professionals. They shouldn't be coerced or forced into taking medication and, similarly, they shouldn't be prevented from trying it if they are sure they want to.

Co-existing conditions

The final section of this chapter focuses on something known as 'comorbidities' – a term which implies the existence of two or more medical conditions at the same time, especially those which are closely linked to ADHD. That said, I detest the word comorbidity. While medically the word morbid is used to refer to a disease, most of us will think about people who have an unnatural obsession with death and illnesses – for example, when somebody has 'a morbid fascination' with something unpleasant. As we discussed earlier in this chapter, the idea that ADHD is a disorder is uncomfortable for many, and associating this with even more medicalised language related to diseases is not a positive way for parents, carers or children to think about it. For this reason, I prefer to use the term 'co-existing conditions'.

More than two-thirds of those diagnosed with ADHD have at least one other co-existing condition and it is, therefore, highly likely that your child does, too. Perhaps you are already aware of this, or maybe the idea is new to you. If you fall into the latter category, then I hope a quick whistlestop tour of some common conditions that co-exist with ADHD will help you to better understand and support your child.

Autism and AuDHD

Over 20 per cent of children with ADHD are also autistic.[9] When autism and ADHD co-exist, the common terminology used is AuDHD. While autism and ADHD are distinct neurodevelopmental conditions, they can share some similarities, such as struggles with emotion regulation, sleep, hyper-focus and executive functions. They differ when it comes to challenges in social situations. For instance, autistic children may have difficulties understanding social cues, communication and relationships, whereas children with ADHD will often struggle in social situations because of hyperactive or explosive behaviour or issues with interrupting or spacing out during conversations.

From a sensory perspective, autistic children will often face challenges with heightened or decreased sensory sensitivity and can display sensory-seeking or sensory-avoiding behaviour, whereas children with ADHD may find certain sensory situations challenging because they divert their focus and attention. Often, there are differences relating to time management and perception and the avoidance of or need for routines (for autistic children), or spontaneity (for children with ADHD). Having AuDHD can present unique challenges for children and knowing that at least one in five children with ADHD is also autistic is important for parents and carers to acknowledge if their child is newly diagnosed with ADHD.

Pathological demand avoidance (PDA) and oppositional defiant disorder (ODD)

While these two conditions may initially appear similar, both resulting in children struggling with behaviour that can be perceived as 'defiant' by adults, they are quite different. PDA occurs in autistic children and is categorised by extreme avoidance of everyday demands placed upon them (such as asking them to brush their teeth, tidy their room or put on their shoes). PDA is thought to be rooted in anxiety and a need for more autonomy. ODD, on the other hand, is not viewed as a neurodivergent condition and is categorised by extreme and hostile reactions to those considered to be in authority positions (for instance, teachers and parents). Children with ODD can appear very angry, argumentative and irritable. There is no one clear underlying cause, although it is likely there is an interplay between genetics, temperament and the environment in which a child is raised.

Up to 30 per cent of children diagnosed with ADHD also show signs of PDA[10], while up to half may also show signs of ODD.[11]

Rejection sensitive dysphoria (RSD)

RSD makes children (and adults) more sensitive to the thoughts and feelings of others. This is especially related to fears of rejection, which, when perceived, can lead to intense emotional reactions. RSD is essentially a sign of extreme emotion dysreg-ulation. RSD affects a huge number of individuals with ADHD, if not all. In fact, it is often considered as a main symptom, and perhaps rather than viewing it as a co-existing condition, it would be better to think of it as a core part of ADHD. Given how common it is for an individual with ADHD to experience RSD, it always surprises me that so few are aware of its existence.

Learning disabilities

Learning disabilities such as dyslexia (affecting reading, writ-ing and spelling), dyscalculia (affecting number understanding and manipulation) and dyspraxia (affecting movement and co-ordination) are fairly common in children diagnosed with ADHD. It is estimated that between one quarter and one half of children with ADHD also have a learning difficulty.[12] This can make education even more challenging for children affected and can increase some more explosive signs of ADHD, as children struggle not only with their attention and regulating their behaviour, but their understanding of and engagement with lessons, too.

Sensory processing disorder (SPD)

Up to 40 per cent of children with ADHD may also have SPD.[13] SPD affects the child's processing of sensory inputs when their brain struggles with receiving appropriate information from their different senses. Children are often hypersensitive to sen-sory input, including noise, smells, light and touch, but they can also experience difficulty with hyposensitivity and seek and crave more sensory input. This sensory-seeking behaviour can mimic the hyperactivity sometimes seen in ADHD; however, the underlying cause is very different.

Misophonia and synaesthesia

Both misophonia and synaesthesia involve differences in sensory processing.

Misophonia affects an individual's tolerance of certain sounds, resulting in a heightened emotional response to a specific noise – for instance, hearing another person chewing food can trigger extreme anger, or even fear. Misophonia is thought to affect around 3 per cent of all individuals.[14] However, many people with ADHD struggle with hypersensitivity to sounds and the incidence of misophonia, therefore, is likely to be higher in children with ADHD.

Synaesthesia is a condition where the brain processes sensory information through multiple or different cognitive pathways in the brain. For instance, an individual may be able to hear colours or smell words. Synaesthesia affects between 2 and 4 per cent of the general population, but is more common in neurodivergent individuals, and research has indicated that it may be caused by hyperexcitability in certain areas of the brain.[15]

Anxiety and depression

Rates of anxiety in children have been rising steeply, with a recent review suggesting that it affects 19 per cent of children and adolescents today.[16] Children with ADHD, however, are significantly more likely to be anxious than their neurotypical peers, with indicators that around 35 per cent have clinically diagnosable anxiety.[17]

Similarly, levels of depression in children and adolescents with ADHD are up to 50 per cent higher than in their neurotypical peers.[18] Anxiety and depression can be related to ADHD symptoms; however, the stigma, ostracising, frequent punishments and shaming, and the friendship difficulties experienced by children with ADHD often serve to make things much worse. For these reasons, all parents and carers of children with ADHD should be on high alert for poor mental health.

Language disorders

Language disorders, such as delayed speech and stammering (known as stuttering in the USA), are significantly more common in children with ADHD than in their neurotypical peers. Research has suggested that up to 40 per cent of children with ADHD also have some sort of language disorder.[19] Research has found that children who stammer are three times more likely to have ADHD than those who do not, indicating a clear association between the two.[20] Sadly, stammering can cause even lower self-esteem in children with ADHD, and delayed speech can add to frustrations with communication and emotion regulation, often intensifying dysregulated and explosive behaviour.

Hypermobility

Hypermobility, which many refer to as being 'double-jointed', is a condition that affects the individual's range of movement. Hypermobile people often experience hyperextension of joints, joint instability, sprains and strains and even dislocations. Commonly, hypermobility can result in frequent joint pain and discomfort, especially with day-to-day movements that many take for granted, like holding a pen and writing. Children with hypermobility often have poor handwriting skills as a result. There is a significant link between ADHD and hypermobility, with research indicating neurodivergent individuals are more than twice as likely as neurotypical people to be hypermobile.[21]

What should you do if you think your child may have a co-existing condition?

If you recognise your child in any of these descriptions or sus-pect that they may be experiencing a co-existing condition, please trust your instinct. If you already have a consultant paediatrician, then take notes and raise your concerns at your child's next appointment. You could also book an appointment with your family doctor and ask for a specialist referral or speak with the SENCo if your child attends school. The chances of your child having a co-existing condition are high, and seeking an appropriate diagnosis and support is key in helping them to thrive. Too many children with ADHD live with co-existing conditions that are never diagnosed.

I hope that you have found this chapter useful, though perhaps sometimes challenging, in exploring ADHD diagnoses, medica-tion and co-existing conditions. While the best route for you and your child is the one that feels most natural and comfortable for you all, I make no attempt to hide how pro-diagnosis I am. As I mentioned earlier in this chapter, while many view a diagnosis as an 'unnecessary label', I view it as an essential one – because if children don't receive an ADHD label, they will receive a far more derogatory one, or, even worse, choose a hurtful one for themselves.

It really is time to end the stigma that surrounds a neurodiver-gence diagnosis and this is a pertinent point to close this chapter on, before we pick up on it again in the next one, which is all about the myths and misconceptions of ADHD in our society today.

Chapter Two

Myth busting and conspiracy theories

'Have you tried putting him on an organic, additive-free, unprocessed vegan diet?'

'It's the screens and not enough nature. Take away his phone, encourage free play and get him into forest school.'

'Try omega-3 oil, mushrooms and aromatherapy oil. Also chiropractic.'

If I hear one more comment like this, I think I may actually scream. I know that most people just want to help, and they likely fully believe in the efficacy of their suggestions, but these sorts of comments are infuriating, as I'm sure you know all too well.

If you're like me, you've probably tried everything (and I really do mean everything), too. There is not a 'treatment', technique or tip that I have not tried. Over the years, I have spent thousands of pounds and a similar number of hours researching, purchasing, preparing and trying the latest suggestion to help my son. The one problem all these supposedly helpful suggestions have in common is the erroneous assumption that you can 'cure' ADHD and explosive behaviour. Sure, there are many things that may make symptoms worse, or better (and I am not attacking or belittling these), but they don't cause the ADHD or dysregulated behaviour and therefore they can't remove it either. The other issue here, of course, is that all these approaches are highly ableist – that is, they all treat ADHD and explosive behaviour as a disease that needs to be cured to make the child 'normal' or neurotypical. I'm all for anything that can take the edge off a little and help both the child and their parents or carers, but these always have to come from a position of acceptance first.

In this chapter I want to walk you through some of the most common myths, misconceptions and downright conspiracy theories I hear about children with ADHD and explosive behaviour. We will consider the evidence behind these ideas, which may be helpful, or indeed harmful, before ending on a discussion as to how you can tackle these conversations when you find yourself in the middle of them.

'ADHD is just a made-up label for naughty children and poor parenting'

One of the hardest things for parents and carers to deal with is the way that others view and understand their child, compared to the reality. While we may know that ADHD is a hereditary neurodevelopmental disorder, and that explosive behaviour is an indication that the child is neurologically dysregulated, others unfortunately still believe it's just an excuse for naughty children in need of more discipline (and for discipline, read punishment).

I have come across real pushback lately from many childcare and therapy professionals concerning what they deem 'the

over-labelling of children'. These beliefs usually end with a comment along the lines of: 'We need to stop labelling children with
ADHD, OCD, PDA and any other ABC they can think of.' These
comments undermine the diagnoses, conditions and lived experiences of families and instead insinuate that desperate parents are
grabbing at a set of initials in order to label their children and
abdicate themselves of responsibility for their behaviour. This
view is at best naïve, and at worst parent shaming and ableist.

ADHD and explosive behaviour still carry an enormous
amount of stigma and the view that it is just an excuse for
naughty children and poor parenting is alarmingly common. In
the next chapter we will discuss why your child's behaviour is
not their fault, but it's not your fault either (something we focus
on in Chapter Nine), and yet this misconception places blame
on both the child and their parents. Not only is this unhelpful,
potentially adding to the shame, guilt and feelings of inadequacy
many parents and their children already struggle with, it can
also make the parents more likely to use harsh discipline on
their children.

Research has shown that children with ADHD are more often
on the receiving end of overly strict and controlling parenting
techniques, maltreatment and sometimes abuse as a result of
their behaviour and parents struggling to cope, rather than the
parenting causing the condition.[1] The ADHD symptoms and
explosive behaviour are the triggers for the harsh parenting and
potential maltreatment, not vice versa. What we also know is
that the more a parent feels that their child's behaviour is their
fault, the more stressed they become and the more likely they
are to turn to harsh parenting.[2] Then the more hopeless they
feel when these methods inevitably don't work and the more
likely they are to reach a state of parental burnout. Once a
parent hits a state of burnout, it is more probable that they will
become detached and dissociate from their child.[3] This burnout
can also set off a new chain of difficult behaviour, when the

parent themselves becomes highly dysregulated emotionally, which, in turn, can result in more out-of-control behaviour from the child.

What is the answer here? What we need to do is to show acceptance, empathy and compassion for both child and parent – remove the blame, stop ridiculing and judging diagnoses and, instead, direct our energy into giving some actual support.

'ADHD is just an excuse for lazy parents to drug their kids'

I find this one particularly damaging. Why? Not only is it highly judgemental and factually incorrect (the most common theme I find when talking to parents of newly diagnosed children is that they are scared of medication and would rather avoid it), it can cause both children and parents to shun medication because of the gross stigma attached to it. Medication may have been life-changing for them, and yet they avoid it because of the uninformed opinions of people who indicate that there is a large movement of parents who are so lazy that they want to drug their children into quiet obedience and submission, so that they don't have to do their job (of parenting) anymore.

The assumption that the medication 'turns children into zombies' is a huge one online and is also entirely incorrect, as this is not remotely how it works (see page 28). Many detractors will also talk about the 'over-medicalisation of children these days' and how easy it is to get them on medication. While it may be relatively easy to do this in countries with mainly private healthcare, such as the USA, this is simply not the case in the UK, where parents will often wait for years within the NHS to reach the point of seeing a medical professional who will consider (with no guarantee) prescribing medication for their child. In the USA, the Center for Disease Control estimates that 69 per cent of children diagnosed with ADHD are taking prescription medication for it; in the UK, this sits at 62 per cent.⁴ Perhaps a more appropriate question to ask here is why are more than a third of children diagnosed with a neurodevelopmental condition *not* in receipt of medication that can be highly effective and helpful for them? Can you imagine any other condition where a third of children weren't prescribed pharmaceutical treatment that could potentially be life-changing? There would be an uproar, not because two-thirds of them had a prescription for it, but because a third of them didn't. Why is this different when it comes to ADHD? Again, we come back to the stigma and the judgemental beliefs that the medication is an excuse for 'bad parenting'.

'ADHD is just an excuse for parents to claim free benefit payments'

There are approximately 14.5 million children in the UK at the time of writing and, according to the National Institute for Health and Care Excellence (NICE), approximately 5 per cent of them have a diagnosis of ADHD; this means that in the UK there are currently around 725,000 children with ADHD.⁵ A recent report found the total number of current Disability Living Allowance (DLA) claims in the UK to be 682,000. However, only approximately 66,000 children (or 9.5 per cent of those diagnosed with ADHD) receive disability-related benefit payments because of their ADHD. In other countries, this figure is even lower; in some, it is non-existent. Even if a child is in receipt of the highest levels of DLA (which is rare for an ADHD diagnosis), the amount paid by the UK government is less than 30 per cent of the UK's average monthly wage. Considering many parents of children with ADHD find themselves having to move to part-time work or give up their job entirely to care for their child or provide them with an education at home, this is not an attractive prospect financially.

I had no idea I could have claimed DLA for Flynn. Nobody told me, I didn't receive any booklets or handouts that explained what governmental help may be available for us, despite having to reduce my workload to cope. It was only when I started to volunteer for the charity Citizens Advice, a few years after his diagnosis, that I found out there was a benefit payment we would have been entitled to. We did go on to claim Personal Independence Payment (PIP), which is a sort of adult version of DLA. The money went directly to him, to help him fund reasonable adjustments to enable him to live more independently when he was at university, but even that took a whole year to process, with a huge amount of fighting and effort. Our first application was declined and so was our second (known as a 'mandatory reconsideration'). Our final chance was to appeal the Department for Work and Pension's (DWP) decision by taking them to court. Finally, after attending a court tribunal hearing, where we gave evidence and spoke to independent experts, we managed to overturn the DWP's decision that he wasn't entitled to PIP. There was no celebration when he 'won' the court case – just a sour taste and regret at having to make use of the British legal system in order to get Flynn what he was entitled to all along. I was fortunate that my training at Citizens Advice had prepared me for the fight, but many do not have the information that I did, and so their claims are dropped and their young adults never receive the financial help they need.

Therefore, when I hear people claiming that parents only get their children diagnosed to get 'free money', my response is an eye roll and a muttering of 'If only they knew . . .' – because they quite clearly haven't tried to navigate our social-security system with a child with ADHD.

'ADHD is overdiagnosed these days'

'So many more children have ADHD today; it can't be a real thing . . .' 'Parents just want to get their children diagnosed with anything nowadays . . .'

I have overhead so many comments like these while on public transport, in cafes and, sadly, at school parents' evenings. While it is true that there has been a dramatic increase in the number of ADHD diagnoses over the last decade, the majority are in adults, not children.[6] Between 2000 and 2018, for instance, diagnosis of ADHD in adults increased twentyfold. Child diagnoses did increase, too, but only moderately in comparison.[7]

Even if diagnoses are increasing, we must not be too quick to conclude that it is overdiagnosed, or indeed, that it is on the rise. The most obvious explanation here is that individuals with ADHD have always existed; they were just 'the naughty ones', 'the weird ones', 'the difficult ones', 'the dreamers' or 'the ones who could never keep still'. There is a reason why the rate of diagnoses is increasing so much in adults, as people finally learn that they are neurodivergent and that the difficulties they faced during childhood were not their fault. The more we, as adults, speak freely about our mental health and our challenges, the more open we are to looking into possible neurodivergence. Combine this interest in mental health with increased awareness of ADHD and access to private healthcare and diagnostic services and the so-called 'increase' is easily explained.

When it comes to childhood diagnoses, the advent of social media discussion groups, and parenting styles that place a focus on neuroscience, such as gentle parenting, it is a natural next step that increased awareness leads parents to seek a diagnosis for their child if they are struggling with their behaviour and feel it is more out of control and explosive than that of their neurotypical peers. It's not that more children have ADHD, it's just that we're better these days at identifying it and talking about it, as well as less willing to force children to be something they're not.

'ADHD is caused by childhood vaccinations'

This myth is largely based on an erroneous belief, prevalent in the early 1990s, that autism was caused by the MMR (measles, mumps and rubella) vaccination given to babies. This viewpoint, which quickly became the hot topic of conversation in parent-and-baby groups, was based on a study that was later proved to be fraudulent and withdrawn by the *Lancet*, the journal in which it was published.[8] Despite thoroughly debunking the research as a whole, there was a shred of truth in one of the underlying beliefs – that thimerosal (a mercury-containing preservative used in vaccines between the 1930s and early 2000s) may be linked to neurodevelopmental disorders. Mercury is a known neurotoxin, meaning that it can alter the structure or function of the developing brain. Vaccines containing thimerosal have, however, been phasing out for the past two decades, and it is not contained in any of the routine vaccines babies or young children receive today in the UK or the USA. A child born in 1999, at the height of the MMR vaccine and autism fears, would have been subject to 200 micrograms of mercury from their infant vaccines, whereas a child born in 2010 is subject to less than 3 micrograms.[9] Removing thimerosal from childhood vaccines has not reduced the incidence of ADHD, quite the contrary, as we have previously discussed in this chapter rates have increased since the action.

'ADHD is just undiagnosed childhood trauma'

This is a tricky one, as there is a correlation between traumatic childhood events and diagnoses of ADHD and explosive behaviour as children grow. However, correlations are not causations. We already know that children with ADHD are more likely to be on the receiving end of maltreatment because of their behaviour (not vice versa) and we know that parents of children with ADHD are more prone to face burnout and experience their own dysregulated behaviour and disconnect from their children, as well as being significantly more likely to be neurodivergent themselves. In essence, it is possible that ADHD increases the incidence of childhood trauma.

We also know that individuals with ADHD have changes in the amygdalae in their brains, as well as other areas responsible for emotion regulation and impulse control, and this can cause them to struggle more with situations that they may find triggering or traumatic. The question here is: is it the trauma that triggers the ADHD and explosive behaviour or the ADHD that triggers the exaggerated response to a potentially traumatic event? I think it is the latter. Changes to the brain of an individual with ADHD can be observed in infancy, via twin studies and, most importantly in the case of trauma, adoption studies show that nature has a stronger influence than nurture on the wiring of the ADHD brain.

Does this mean that trauma does not make behaviour worse, increasing ADHD-type symptoms? Absolutely not. It is logical to assume that it does. Similarly, trauma can also produce ADHD-like behaviour problems in neurotypical children, but this doesn't mean that they have ADHD – more that their trauma response masquerades as ADHD. There are certainly links between trauma and behaviour, not only that which is explosive, but that which is not externalised; for instance, apparent inattentiveness may actually be dissociation due to underlying trauma. Again, in this case it would be wrong to diagnose this dissociation as ADHD.

It makes sense that those working in therapy-related roles with a focus on childhood trauma see many children with behavioural traits that are similar to those of children with ADHD, but to say that all ADHD is caused by childhood trauma is not only incorrect, but potentially dangerous, as it can make parents reluctant to seek a diagnosis, medication or other related help and also means they may not be as legally protected (for instance, in the education system) as they should be. I don't believe these therapists want parents and children to go without something that could help them, but this, unfortunately, is often what their opinions lead to.

All the beliefs we have discussed so far in this chapter are easy to debunk with ample evidence. Where it gets a little trickier to dismiss a belief, however, is where there is an element of truth that is mixed with an equal or greater measure of confusion. It is true that many things can make explosive behaviour and other symptoms of ADHD more out of control, whereas others may help to improve them. While we are discussing this, however, it is important to understand that they are palliating symptoms, not curing them (or indeed causing them). As ever, all children are different. What works to regulate some does not work for others. When something does have a positive effect, just remember it is not your unique child that it is changing, but rather their externalised behaviour.

'ADHD is caused by toxic chemical exposure'

In a world of Instagram and TikTok influencers, interest in chemical-laden household products that promise shiny sinks, gleaming floors, fresh-smelling laundry and highly scented homes is surging at an alarming pace. I was shocked to watch one video recently in which a heavily scented disinfectant was being used as a room freshener. These products have a huge, almost cult-like, following among mothers of young families and I have always wondered what the effect is on babies (including in utero) and toddlers who grow up surrounded by clouds of artificial scents.

There is a rising body of evidence linking household chemicals (including those contained in cleaning products, paint, room scents, carpets and fire-retardant soft furnishings) with neurotoxic effects.[10] Similarly, phthalates and bisphenol, found in some drinking bottles and plastic and vinyl toys, are known endocrine disruptors (chemicals that interfere with the way the body's hormones work), which can impact the development of dopamine receptors (an area we know shows differences in those with ADHD) in the brains of babies still in the womb. Indeed, there is some research indicating an increased risk of developing ADHD in children exposed to these substances.[11] Does this mean that ADHD is solely caused by chemical exposure? Doubtful. The strong hereditary link clearly shows us that there is a genetic predisposition at play, but perhaps these children are more susceptible to the effects of certain chemicals, particularly in utero. Maybe avoidance of them may lessen symptoms, too. If it does, though, we shouldn't perceive living a more chemical-free lifestyle as 'a cure', merely as something of an amelioration of symptoms. We would all do well to reduce our usage of neurotoxic chemicals around our homes, especially if we have young children.

'ADHD is actually a sleep disorder'

I have been reading lots of articles suggesting that ADHD is just the external manifestation of sleep-disordered breathing, or specifically mouth breathing and sleep apnoea (characterised by the repeated temporary stopping of breathing during sleep). While there is undeniably a strong link between ADHD and sleep disorders, and research shows that up to half of all children with ADHD have related sleep difficulties, this association is not necessarily a causation.[12]

Studies of children diagnosed with sleep apnoea, often related to enlarged adenoids (a major cause of mouth breathing during sleep), show that up to 95 per cent display hyperactive behaviour that is similar to that seen in children diagnosed with ADHD. However, the incidence found in children with ADHD sits at somewhere between 20 and 30 per cent, indicating a correlation, rather than a causation.[13] If a child is grossly sleep deprived, their behaviour will be worse, and in the case of sleep apnoea it may be that adults perceive a child to have ADHD when, in fact, the underlying issue is gross overtiredness and sleep deprivation.

The presence of 'ADHD-like' symptoms is different from saying that sleep apnoea or mouth breathing cause ADHD. Does this mean I am saying that seeking medical help for your child's sleep will not have a positive impact on their behaviour? Absolutely not. I'm just arguing the position that sleep issues are not the cause of ADHD. In Chapter Seven we will look at the many ways sleep can impact behaviour and how ADHD can impact sleep, because – in short – every child's behaviour is better if they are well rested.

'ADHD is caused by poor diet'

How many times have you heard the statement 'Kids today are so poorly behaved because they live on a diet of junk, sugar, additives and ultra-processed food'? If you post in an internet discussion forum, or on a social media site asking for help with your child's behaviour, particularly if they are violent or hyperactive, you can guarantee that within the first handful of comments, somebody will suggest that you change their diet. But while there is evidence to suggest that diet impacts behaviour, it isn't *the* cause of it, and nor is it *the* solution.

The long-held myth of 'sugar highs' has been busted time and again with research showing that sugar does not make children hyperactive, and neither do sugar substitutes.[14] Despite many believing that sugar is a major culprit for out-of-control explosive behaviour, again research shows this just isn't the case; it also doesn't negatively impact sleep as so many parents commonly believe.[15] While eating too much sugar clearly isn't good for anybody, the links with sugar and negative behaviour seem to exist largely in the minds of parents and those who advise them, rather than in reality. If an effect is seen on behaviour around sugary foods, it is likely due to the excitement of the environment surrounding them (for instance, a party or other special occasion), or the novelty of being allowed to eat sugar that isn't contained in the child's everyday diet. Of course, there is also likely a nocebo effect at play, in that parents who suspect their child's behaviour will regress after eating sugar are more likely to look for behaviour that that they are not happy with once their child has done so.

Surprisingly, there is a fair body of research showing that consumption of sugar can improve behaviour in childhood, especially when it comes to increasing attention spans and focus at school.[16] When we consider the high metabolic needs of the developing brain and the fuel provided by glucose, it makes sense that sugar may actually palliate, rather than stimulate explosive behaviour and hyperactivity. An adult brain uses around a quarter of consumed glucose for brain processes; however, a child's brain uses up to 40 per cent of their daily glucose intake.[17] Does this mean that food, or specifically ultra-processed food (UPF), does not impact behaviour? Sadly, it's not so simple. Certain additives are definitely linked with poor behaviour and hyperactivity, but again they are not 'the cause'.

There is rising concern, however, surrounding the diets our children consume today. Research has found that British children are currently consuming up to two-thirds of their daily calorie intake from UPFs.[18] The impact of this is sobering, with rising levels of obesity and a potentially ticking cardiac time bomb; UPFs also contain high levels of additives, including artificial colours and flavourings, some of which have been linked to hyperactive behaviour in children.[19] We would all do well to reduce UPFs in our diets; however, it is not a magic solution for stopping explosive behaviour, nor is it a cure for ADHD, and the healthiest approach to diet in childhood (and indeed any age) is one that focuses on moderation, rather than restriction.

'ADHD only really affects boys'

There is a pervasive myth in our society that ADHD is just 'naughty boys', or rather, a condition that solely affects males. This isn't true. While boys are between two and a half and four times more likely to receive a diagnosis than girls, this doesn't necessarily mean more boys are affected.[20] In spotting and diagnosing ADHD, adults tend to look for symptoms that are more obvious in boys, such as explosive behaviour. Girls tend to present differently and are very often missed, not receiving a diagnosis until well into adulthood. It is likely that there are just as many women living with ADHD as there are men today, but the majority are not diagnosed.

There is also a gender bias when it comes to diagnosing girls, with health professionals overlooking the struggles of girls and focusing instead on stereotypical male hyperactive behaviour. This bias also results in girls receiving reduced referrals to ADHD specialists; as we discussed in the previous chapter, girls often present in a very different way to boys, with far fewer receiving a diagnosis.[21]

'ADHD is caused by too much screen time'

The current trend in parenting seems to be an intense focus on demonising screen time. It feels as if every problem children and teens have is blamed on smartphones, social media, gaming, PCs and television. I, for one, am not on board with this witch hunt. If you're reading this book, by now you've probably already realised that screen time quite likely helps your child to self-regulate: in the midst of feeling overwhelmed, overstimulated, anxious, lonely, frustrated or angry, time spent in front of a screen, particularly gaming, can really help neurodivergent children.

Insinuating that all 'poor' behaviour is caused by too much time online is naïve and shows a clear lack of understanding of the importance of screens to many neurodivergent children and their parents. Yes, too much of anything, including screen time, is bad, but like with most things in life, the true answer is a shade of nuanced grey, rather than a black and white prescription of 'all screens are bad' or 'all screens are good'. Families need to find a balance that works for them and their children.

That said, it is true that screen time can also have a negative effect on children's behaviour and excessive use has been linked to increased levels of anxiety, depression, sleep disorders and aggressive and antisocial behaviour.[22] I am always interested in the causality implied in this research, however, and question how much of it is a correlation – in other words, how many children who struggle to regulate their emotions are drawn to screens as a way to self-regulate, rather than the screens themselves being the cause of the problem behaviour and feelings? It's an interesting thought and one I feel is sorely missing from current screen-free child discussion's.

'Complementary therapies can cure ADHD'

Breathwork, CBD oil (cannabis without the THC, the psycho-active component), chiropractic, dietary supplements (including, but not limited to, ginseng, omega-3, mushrooms, sea moss, spirulina and zinc), EFT (tapping), homeopathy, osteopathy, meditation, reflexology, reiki, retained-reflex-release bodywork, yoga . . . You name it, I tried it. If I read an article or an account from somebody claiming that a certain complementary therapy had helped their child, it became my mission to research and source it for Flynn. Most had no impact, short of draining our already stretched finances. Some helped to take the edge off his hyperactivity and explosive behaviour and others (such as omega-3 and zinc) do have limited scientific evidence supporting their use.[23]

For me, I think the most beneficial impact lay in feeling there was something that I could do to help; the search for a 'miracle cure' helped to take away some of the feelings of hopelessness and uselessness that I had been feeling for so long. However, I realised that I was holding an ableist view – one which saw my child as a problem to fix, rather than accepting him for who he was. Perhaps some of these complementary therapies help your child, perhaps you practise them for yourself, perhaps you're even a practitioner. I'm not saying there is any issue with doing any of the things I've listed in this section (or others I haven't). If they help your child, that's brilliant. I think we just have to move away from the idea of 'fixing' children, especially with therapies that can be incredibly expensive and marketed at exhausted and desperate parents in such a way that promises 'solutions'.

'Everybody is on the spectrum somewhere!'

'Everybody is a little bit ADHD, aren't they?' Perhaps you have heard this one? I hear it a lot, and often it is said in a way that implies the person is dismissive of ADHD. The reality, however, is that everybody isn't 'a little bit ADHD'. You either have it or you don't. It may be the case that some people have certain of its traits, even though they do not have it, but ADHD is not a normal curve of distribution, or a spectrum on which you can plot the whole of the population.

'ADHD is a superpower' – or is it?

This is one other belief that I would like to discuss and it's a contentious one. In fact, you may be surprised to see it in this section at all, instead believing that I am somebody who upholds, even champions it. It is the suggestion that ADHD is a superpower – an idea that I find deeply uncomfortable.

I understand completely the need to lift our children up and help them to recognise how amazing they are (we'll talk about this lots later in this book). What I am not a fan of is toxic positivity and spinning a developmental disorder, or indeed something classified as a disability, as 'a superpower'. This is all well and good if the child is not struggling and fits into society's expectations well, but when they don't, it can leave them feeling even more ostracised than they are already. ADHD is not a superpower and to imply that it is can grossly underestimate the discrimination that individuals (both children and adults) face.

The other issue with the idea of possessing superpowers is that it pressures children with ADHD to strive to be 'extra' – to achieve more and work harder than their peers in order to be accepted. This is an ableist idea (ableism is the discrimination of those who are not able-bodied, or neurotypical) because it does not accept the children for who they are. I'm sure parents who use the superhero analogy don't mean to pile more pressure on to their children, but that is unfortunately what happens when it is used.

Am I saying that there are no benefits to having ADHD? Absolutely not. I'm all about reframing it and focusing on the positives (you'll see some in the boxed text after this section). Similarly, I think it's so important to share inspiring stories with children about people who have an ADHD diagnosis and have gone on to accomplish amazing things in their lives (again, you can see some in the boxed text shortly), but dismissing lived struggles and pretending those with ADHD are superheroes is not helpful, and it's something I have always avoided.

One idea I can get strongly behind, though, is the idea that ADHD is an evolutionary advantage. Research suggests that traits of ADHD may have helped foraging in hunter-gatherer society, with those individuals more likely to walk off and try different things, resulting in better foraging and gaining more food for the tribe or family.[24] Those who were better at searching for food, particularly in areas where it was sparse, would not only help their own survival, but that of their tribe, too. Researchers tested this hypothesis with an online simulation where participants (some with diagnosed ADHD, some not) were asked to 'forage', while the computer timed how long it took them to deplete resources from areas sparse in food. Participants with ADHD did so quicker and were more likely to explore other areas than neurotypical participants who tended to stay in the sparse areas for longer. ADHD may not be a superpower, but it may have helped to feed our ancestors and played a key role in our evolution as a species.

CELEBRITIES WITH ADHD

- Simone Biles – Olympic gymnast
- Michael Phelps – Olympic swimmer
- Nicola Adams – Olympic boxer
- Ryan Gosling – actor
- Jamie Oliver – chef
- will.i.am – musician
- Greta Gerwig – director and actor
- Bill Gates – founder of Microsoft
- Ant McPartlin – presenter
- Ben Fogle – journalist
- Sheridan Smith – actor
- Dav Pilkey – author and cartoonist
- Ellen DeGeneres – television host
- Lewis Hamilton – racing driver
- Sir Richard Branson – entrepreneur
- Tom Hanks – actor
- Stephen Hawking – theoretical physicist
- Stephen Fry – broadcaster

POSITIVE TRAITS OF INDIVIDUALS WITH ADHD

- Adventurous
- Creative
- Empathetic
- Flexible
- Imaginative
- Spontaneous

- Quick-thinking
- Able to hyper-focus
- Resilient
- Sensitive
- Energetic
- Eager
- Innovative
- Willing to take chances
- Multitasking
- Sociable
- Good conversationalists
- Fast workers
- Unconventional
- Boundary pushers
- Entrepreneurial

How to handle unsolicited advice and opinions from others

As we come to the close of this chapter, I'd like to leave you with a few pointers and responses you can use the next time you find yourself on the receiving end of unsolicited advice and unwanted opinions from others, perhaps about some of the things we've discussed in this chapter, or another gem not mentioned.

I've come to realise that most people are only trying to help. Often, they will phrase this help in a strange, indeed, unhelpful way, but I choose to believe that most tips come from the goodness of people's hearts because they genuinely want to make a positive impact on your life and that of your child. So I'd recommend always starting with this, however weird, wacky, or potentially insulting their recommendations may be: stop, take a breath and tell yourself, *They think they are helping; they don't mean to be rude.*

Of course, some people are also just hideously misinformed, the saddest of these being adults who are clearly neurodivergent but don't realise it. These are the adults who spent the whole of their childhoods being punished for their behaviour and have grown to believe that they were not only the problem, but that they also deserved the maltreatment. There is so much cognitive dissonance here that you are unlikely to make a chink in their armour. Instead, all you can do is smile and nod and tell yourself that their comments are not about you, or your child, but about the hurt inside them and the terrible way that their parents, carers and professionals treated them as a child.

What is the best way to respond to opinions and advice? I can tell you that arguably the worst way is the one that many choose – to jump in with evidence to disprove someone's points and quickly descend into an argument. So many people hold such deeply conditioned beliefs that you won't change their minds, however many clinical studies or statistics you throw at them, and you will quickly find yourself angry, despondent, frustrated and stressed. It is not worth spoiling your peace of mind (especially when the key, perhaps, to parenting a child with ADHD or explosive behaviour is staying as calm as possible yourself – lots on this in Chapter Ten). Instead, my advice is to smile, nod and say, 'Thanks for that, I will consider it' and quickly change the subject. The other person will feel heard, but you have sent a very clear message that you are not open to any further conversation on the matter. If they try to raise their point again, then be more direct, saying, 'Thank you. I will think about what you've said, but I do not want to discuss it further with you now.' This has never failed for me.

Maybe when you're feeling stronger, and perhaps, like me, you're a few years further along your journey, you'll feel called to re-educate as many people as possible, but today is not the time for that. Your priority should be yourself and your child now; shut out the noise and focus on your family and your wellbeing. The dissenters and disbelievers will, sadly, still be there for you to tackle in the future.

I hope you found this chapter helpful, although I also hope you come across as few of the ideas discussed in it as possible. Thankfully, opinions and understanding of ADHD and explosive behaviour are beginning to change – not as quickly as I would like, but there are definitely glimmers appearing. Hopefully, by the time your child is an adult, the world will be a very different place when it comes to understanding of neurodivergence and tricky behaviour in childhood. Perhaps your child will even be one of the changemakers whose name I can add to the list of inspirational individuals with ADHD in future editions of this book.

I am always drawn to the idea of those with ADHD bringing about evolutional change. My hope is that one day these individuals will not only help to create a world that accepts them but maybe one that values the special skills and viewpoints that those with ADHD bring to society.

Let's now move on to Chapter Three, which is all about addressing the myths and misconceptions we ourselves hold about our children, and why changing the way we think is the first step towards changing the way they behave.

Chapter Three

It's not their fault

know you're probably reading this book because you want advice on how to tackle your child's difficult behaviour, and I promise we're getting there in the next chapter. Before we reach my discipline tips, however, we have to start with an understanding of what children with ADHD or undiagnosed explosive behaviour are capable of changing and controlling. Spoiler: it's a lot less than many believe. Would that change the way you viewed them? Would it change your parenting? I suspect it probably would, which is why dropping the blame is the most important concept to embrace when it comes to disciplining children with ADHD.

It took me many years of heartache trying to change my son, until one day I had a revelation: what if he *couldn't* change? What if all my efforts had been in vain because his behaviour was no more under his control than how his hair grew, or when he might have got an attack of hiccups? Before this epiphany I couldn't understand why he didn't want to change. Surely he would feel better if he wasn't so out of control and constantly on the receiving end of reprimands everywhere he went? In my quest to try to understand the causes of his behaviour, I realised I had always tried to blame him for it in some way; I hadn't ever considered that it wasn't his fault. Then, one day, after yet another meltdown, when he was about twelve, I asked him if he *could* change his behaviour if he wanted to, and he said 'No,' – he 'couldn't'. We both sobbed – he at the thought of finally being understood, me at the memories of the constant (inevitably failed) attempts I had made to change him and the stress I had put him through in the process.

When I run behaviour and discipline workshops with parents of toddlers, a large amount of time is spent helping them to understand that they are not raising some sort of Machiavellian mini dictator, who spends all day plotting how to wind them up and cause as much heartache and work for them as possible. It's always surprised me quite how much adults perceive toddlers to be fully in control of their behaviour, especially after lengthy attempts to reason with them, or sending them to time out or the naughty step where we mistakenly believe that they will think about their actions, consider how they have impacted others and make a plan to behave better in the future. In fact, when we punish toddlers in this way, all that happens is that they learn that if they sit quietly, the punishment is over quicker; they learn that their parents aren't a safe space for them to be authentic and, ultimately, that they are only lovable when they are not a bother to anybody. In my workshops I use an analogy of a fish riding a bicycle. I ask the parents if they had a pet fish and bought it a bicycle, what do they think would happen? They usually look at me with a 'what-is-this-woman-talking-about?' squint and say, 'Err, that's silly. Of course fish can't ride bikes.' Expecting a toddler to not tantrum is akin to expecting a fish to be able to ride a bicycle. Neither is physiologically equipped to succeed at the task. A toddler's brain is still two decades away from being able to fully control their emotions and in the meantime, our expectations are not only unrealistic, but almost as laughable as the idea of a fish riding a bicycle. The thing is, the parents quickly understand and from that moment on, I feel a weight lifting in the room, as they let out a long-held breath, societally ingrained beliefs about their inability to be 'a good parent' and a whole lot of guilt for the way they have treated their toddler for something that was entirely out of their control. If I was in a room with you now, we would be looking at an A2-sized picture of a goldfish riding a bicycle, as I explained that the fish was your child (even though they may have long grown out of toddlerhood) and the expectation of being able to control their behaviour was as unrealistic as the picture in front of you.

Once you move from a place of never-ending searches for the next behaviour-control hack to one where you realise your child's behaviour is caused by an inability and not a lack of desire to change, then your whole world, and your relationship with your child, transforms. Does this mean I'm saying there is absolutely nothing you can do to improve their behaviour? No, but lower those expectations – you're not going to have an Insta-perfect 'angel child' (and, actually, neither should you want one; I'm always concerned about children who are portrayed as being calm, happy and obedient all the time – it usually means a great deal of masking and emotion avoidance and distraction are happening). There are, however, things you can do with your child to help to take the edge off a little, which we'll cover more in the next chapter – and for those moments when even these don't help, we'll look at what you can do when nothing seems to work in Chapter Five.

The key to not only surviving but thriving in your relation-ship with your child and helping them to be and grow into the happiest and most confident individual is acceptance. Embrace your goldfish and throw away the idea of a bicycle. Perhaps the most damaging thought that parents of children with ADHD and explosive behaviour can hold on to is the idea of what they think life should be like and who they think their child is and should be. The weight of these expectations doesn't just cause misery today – it takes away any joy and peace from tomorrow, too. I'm not expecting you to be able to change your thoughts and dreams for your child overnight; it's taken many years to build them up and it will probably take considerable time for you to learn to fully let them go – and that's OK, as long as you start. You have to accept these children as they are, rather than trying to change them. Meet them where they are, rather than having a goal to change their behaviour. Once you drop ideas of deliberate defiance, manipulation and naughtiness and instead move to a place of 'perhaps they already are doing the best they can', everything is different. When they feel safe to be authentically themselves and know that you're on their side, that's where the magic happens.

How do children with explosive behaviour feel?

If your child is old enough to verbalise their feelings to you, I'd highly recommend taking a break from this book for a moment and asking them how they feel when their behaviour is dysregulated and they're out of control. Ask them what goes through their mind immediately before they do something inappropriate. How do they feel during a meltdown and what do they think about afterwards? I suspect you'll be surprised at their answers. I was when I asked my son. In fact, here's his reply to me:

> I thought everybody else felt the same as me and that everybody struggled. I didn't realise I was different. Whenever I did something bad there was no thought process behind it; it was just something I did. I can't ever remember a time that I plotted to do something naughty. If I was told to not do something by somebody that didn't help, as in my head I was already going to do it and I didn't have the power

> to stop myself. It was like my brain just made me do
> things and I couldn't stop it. I didn't think about the
> repercussions. Even if I could see the bad outcomes,
> thinking about any consequences didn't help. When
> the thought to do something was in my head, there
> wasn't really very much anybody could have done
> to stop me. Even if I knew something was wrong, I
> couldn't help it.
>
> When I was very out of control, with lots of anger,
> I remember feeling like I needed to hit something.
> My anger can go from zero to one hundred very
> quickly and I had to do something to get rid of the
> anger, rather than sitting with it. There is nothing that
> could have helped me to calm down at the time, I
> don't think. As I've got older, I can calm down now by
> spending time alone – sometimes I play video games
> to help, but when I was younger, I would get stuck in a
> meltdown-and-anger cycle for hours.

When he was a child, I always struggled to understand the destructiveness of Flynn's behaviour. I have raised all my children in an anti-violent, gentle way, to be respectful of others and people's property and belongings. This seemed to work well with my other three children, but for Flynn something was different. We live in a very old house, with old lime and horsehair plaster and lots of oak beams, and the four-hundred-year-old plaster is quite fragile. Flynn's meltdowns would often see him stomping on the floor in his bedroom. He did this so much that the ceiling of the room beneath his bedroom began to cave in. For about a year, we had a big hole in the ceiling and it felt pointless to repair it because we knew it would just happen again. Instead, we just nailed a piece of plywood over it as a temporary measure, hoping that the violent outbursts would end and we could then repair the ceiling properly – something we finally did when

Flynn was around sixteen. The mismatched, patched plaster is still a reminder today of what he experienced, like a scar our house bears as an illustration of our familial heartache. If only I had truly understood, I would have encouraged him to let off steam safely downstairs, or in our garden. Instead, I tried – again and again – to talk him out of his rage, distract him from it, or try every new calming technique on the block to prevent the outbursts. All these attempts naturally failed.

We mustn't view anger as bad; it is just an emotion. In my other parenting books, I speak a lot about the importance of emodiversity, which is the valuing of all feelings. Here, the issue was with the manifestation of anger and how Flynn handled it, not the actual anger itself. My efforts to stop the anger, rather than helping him to release it in a less destructive way, were the issue and the one thing, ultimately, that I had control of.

Flynn's impulsivity was also something we struggled with a lot when he was younger. He seemed to have little concept of danger or safety. As he said himself, once he got a thought in his head about doing something there was little he could do to ignore it. One incident that still stands out in my mind occurred when he was at secondary school, shortly after being diagnosed with ADHD. I received a phone call from the school around midday saying: 'Mrs Ockwell-Smith, Flynn has picked and eaten some unidentified berries. Can you please come and pick him up and take him to the hospital accident and emergency department.' Thankfully, I'm a keen forager and gardener and quickly identified the berries as hawthorn – not the tastiest of berries, but not poisonous either, so a hospital visit was ruled out. When I asked what had happened, Flynn said that they had been having a PE lesson out on the school field. He'd spotted some berries, thought they looked tasty, so decided to walk off and harvest them (despite having no clue what they were). His teacher spotted him several minutes later and panicked, hence the call to me. After the event, he could discuss firstly, why it was a bad idea to forage alone if he didn't know what he was picking and secondly, why it also was not a good idea to walk away from a school PE lesson. At the time, however, this knowledge was not enough to override his impulsivity. I could have been angry with him, but what was the point? In the end, what I took the most from the experience was the need to educate him more about foraging safety and the school about closer supervision during outside lessons. It was nobody's fault – not Flynn's, the school's or mine – but we all needed to learn something from what happened. Punishment wouldn't achieve anything here and, thankfully, we didn't have any further unplanned foraging!

While I was researching this book, I was fortunate enough to speak to some children who had either an ADHD diagnosis or a suspected one alongside explosive behaviour. I asked them to tell me how it feels when they are dysregulated and feel out of control. This is what they told me:

'It's like having a black circle filled with balls inside you. You don't know what those balls are, you can just feel them bouncing around. So you try and do something with all the energy, so you fidget or chat to your friends or do something you're not meant to. (Also, you're really bored and trying to find something interesting to help you focus.) So then you get told off, and that's embarrassing and makes you angry, which makes the balls go faster and faster.'

'I can't sit still; it makes me feel trapped. Sometimes I need to run to get all my angry out, away from other people. ADHD means I have lots of energy and I like to do sports. I find it really hard to listen and understand people when they talk lots and give me too many questions or instructions.'

'You know in a film about a teenager at school, something embarrassing has happened and all the kids in the hallway are laughing and jeering and it feels like the room is closing in and shrinking towards them with too much noise and sound and stimulation – that's how it feels for me.'

'I know I shouldn't do the things I do and I kind of wish I didn't but it's like something takes over and possesses my brain and I'm not the one in control anymore.'

'When I'm very stressed or angry I can't think straight. Everything buzzes around my head like lots of angry bees and I can only make them go away if I scream. I don't mean to be horrible and I don't like upsetting people. If I could make the bees go away some other way, then I would.'

A common theme

Reading through the quotes above, what struck me was a common theme running through all of them: that they all struggled to control their behaviour. None of them told me that they had deliberately decided to behave in a disruptive or disrespectful manner. Despite this, however, so many children with an ADHD diagnosis or undiagnosed explosive behaviour are threatened, punished, shamed and blamed, as if their behaviour is under their conscious control and is all their own fault.

> ### EXERCISE: HOW DID YOU FEEL?
>
> Can you remember a time as a child when you behaved 'poorly', according to society's standards? In particular, can you remember a time when your behaviour was explosive,

either verbally or physically? I'd like you to take a moment to recall the event. Where were you? Who were you with? What time of day or night was it? What time of year? What was the weather like? Were you inside or outside? How were you feeling? Were you hungry? Tired? Perhaps you felt sick?

Grab a pen and paper or use the notes app on your phone or other device and make a list of all these points. When you've done that, I'd like you to think specifically about your explosive or 'naughty' behaviour. What were you thinking about immediately before you did it? What were you thinking about during the event? How did you feel afterwards? Next, think about how your parents or carers reacted. How did they make you feel? How did you feel half an hour after the event? Or later that day?

I hope the above exercise has helped to give you some insight into how your child feels when they are dysregulated. I always use an example of my own life when I was around four years old. It was close to my birthday and my mother had ordered a cake for my party from a local baker. I can still remember it vividly today. It was the most beautiful thing I had ever seen, with a Sindy doll inserted into the centre, so that the cake looked like her skirt – a huge pale pink ballgown decorated with darker pink piping and flowers (yes, I am a child of the 70s!). I was excited for my birthday, excited for my party and feeling restless and frustrated that I still had so long (a whole day) to wait. I also remember that I was hungry, and as we walked into the bakery, the smell of fresh bread and sausage rolls made me salivate. I was so overcome with excitement, hunger and awe at my cake that I reached up to touch it on the counter and promptly grabbed a small handful out of it. I didn't mean to; it was softer than I'd expected, and I remember my hand sinking in before being met with a swift slap from my mother's. The only thing I remember after that point was pain, anger, rage, and the colour red. I'm pretty sure I threw myself on to the floor of the bakery and I remember hearing people shouting. As the red mist faded, I felt despair, sadness, confusion and overwhelming guilt and shame. I hadn't meant to lunge at the cake; I just couldn't control my hand at the time. There was no malice, no deliberate attempt to destroy this thing of beauty – just a little girl struggling to control her impulses and her hand reacting before her brain switched into gear. I have thought of that little girl often over the last two decades, and my mother, too. We weren't rich. I knew she would have had to have made sacrifices to order me that cake and I know, having been the mother of an out-of-control child, how embarrassed and upset she would have been. The sad thing is, the emotions I felt at the time and those my mother felt were probably identical: embarrassment, anger, sadness and disbelief. There was no need to add punishment to that list. I already knew I had done wrong, and I already felt bad.

If you think about a time when your child has exploded, particularly in public – a time I'm sure you found unbelievably difficult, embarrassing and rage-inducing – and consider how your child felt, it's likely to be similar to how you would have felt as a child. Nobody feels good when they are out of control. Why would your child wish that behaviour on themselves? Why would they choose to be that dysregulated deliberately? Why would they choose the punishments they have undoubtedly been on the receiving end of so often? Why would anybody behave this way on purpose? Can you imagine the impact of being called 'naughty' all the time? Of knowing that people have a low opinion of you? Knowing that teachers are always having to call home about you? And that your parents feel let down? Why would we ever think it's a dysregulated child's 'fault'?

The cycle of shame

Many children with ADHD and undiagnosed explosive behaviour struggle with low levels of self-esteem and confidence. They quickly learn that they aren't 'good enough' and, for some, this can also lead them to believe that they aren't 'loved enough' and are therefore unlovable. This low self-esteem is yet another trigger for difficult behaviour – it's something I call 'the cycle of shame': the child moves from poor behaviour to punishment and feeling shamed, to dented self-esteem, to increasingly dysregulated emotions, which then lead them back to more poor behaviour. This cycle is one that many children find themselves stuck in (perhaps you even remember it from your own childhood?) and, sadly, it can feel impossible to break.

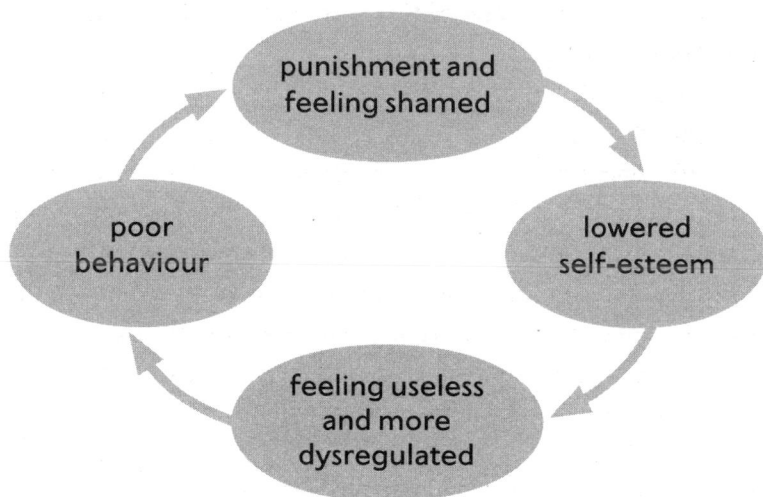

Why we need to drop the word 'naughty'

I suspect that your child has probably been referred to as 'naughty' by several people, perhaps even yourself at times? (I admit, it's slipped my lips on several occasions.) The word 'naughty' is so problematic for all children, but especially for those with ADHD and those who struggle to regulate their behaviour. Why? My top three reasons are:

1. the terrible impact it has on a child's self-esteem
2. because it is factually incorrect and
3. because we are in danger of creating a self-fulfilling prophecy.

Let's look at each of these in a little more detail.

The impact on self-esteem

Labelling a child based on behaviour they cannot control is a sure-fire way to set the cycle of shame in motion. Do you remember when you were a child and somebody called you something derogatory? Perhaps they called you clumsy, said you had two left feet, told you that you were slow or implied you weren't clever. Did it impact your self-esteem and self-belief? Perhaps their words led you to avoid sport or dancing, or perhaps they caused you to believe that you were hopeless at something, so there was no point in trying to improve? The words we use about (and to) our children become the foundations of their self-belief system, not just in childhood, but adulthood, too. If they believe they are naughty, their self-esteem slowly erodes and shame fills the void – and you know where shame leads them to next on the cycle.

The term 'naughty' is factually incorrect

When adults call a child 'naughty', they are implying that the child is in full control of their behaviour and that any difficult behaviour is entirely their own fault. These underlying beliefs, and thus usage of the term, does children a huge disservice by not uncovering or recognising the real cause of the difficult behaviour. As we have discussed already in this chapter, no child wants to be 'naughty'. They are 'naughty' because, in that specific moment in time, they can't behave any better. Motivation isn't a problem; they almost certainly wish they could 'behave'. Using the term 'naughty' sets an adult up on a combative path, where the only acceptable outcome centres on punishing the child in some way for their behaviour.

It is a self-fulfilling prophecy

Labelling helps nobody, least of all the child. The words we use about children can and do change the way we think about them. If we call a child (or their behaviour) 'naughty' enough times, we will start to see them that way, which, subconsciously, changes the way we treat them. Enter the cycle of shame again. And the result? We can unwittingly encourage more of the undesired behaviour because we are constantly on alert for it and because the child, ultimately, learns that this is their role in life. They are 'the naughty one'.

The sooner we lose the word naughty, the better in my view. And the more of us who drop it, hopefully, the fewer will use it in the future.

I was chatting with my son Flynn about the concept of being 'naughty' and how it made him feel to be called it. This is what he said:

*Being called naughty by everybody just made me be-
lieve that was who I was. It made me feel that I wasn't
going to get anywhere in life, that I was a failure, and
that made me less likely to try at school. Eventually,
I became the class clown, shouting things out in lessons, because that was what everybody expected of
me. Other students then encouraged me, which made
things worse. It also took attention away from the fact
I couldn't concentrate on what they were trying to
teach us.*

Is all behaviour communication?

I like the phrase 'all behaviour is communication' because it
makes adults think about the emotions and experiences underlying their child's behaviour. It makes us view the child as an
individual, as human, going through stuff in life. This can make
us more considerate towards them and help spur us on to look for
holistic ways to tackle their behaviour. I do have one big problem
with the phrase, though, and that is that adults can get stuck on
the idea that difficult and explosive behaviour is always about
the child having unmet needs. Sadly, it's not that simple. There is
always a reason for the behaviour, but sometimes (in fact, often)
that reason may just be your child's brain. This is especially true
for brains that are differently wired.

It is deeply frustrating not to be able to pinpoint a cause of the
behaviour, or identify triggers, or even understand why they are
behaving in a certain way. Parents and carers can feel that they
have somehow failed if they cannot correctly identify the source
of a child's behaviour (and rectify it), but everything comes
back to realising that children are unique, with unique brains
(often atypical neurologically) and that their experience of the
world is unique, too. In short, out-of-control behaviour is often

an indicator that something is not right in a child's world, but sometimes it is an indicator of nothing more than their unique brain, and we shouldn't feel disappointed or disheartened if we cannot find a cause. In any case, our response should be the same, regardless of our understanding: to remind ourselves that this is not our child's fault and that at this moment in time, what they need most from us is empathy and support, not chastisement and punishment.

Executive functions – lagging skills

For the remainder of this chapter I'd like to focus on your child's brain and how it may be affecting their behaviour. Let's start with a quick overview of what are known as executive functions.

Executive functions describe the cognitive or mental processes that control an individual's skills relating to decision making, task completion and, importantly for this chapter, emotion regulation. Executive functions act a little like a remote control for a toy robot; they are the drivers of our behaviour, controlling our reactions to situations. Executive functions start to develop in early childhood. However, they do not fully mature until an individual is in their late twenties.

The main executive functions are as follows:

- Flexible thinking – the ability to adapt to different situations by being able to change and revise your thought processes and beliefs
- Emotional control – the ability to understand and regulate your emotions, especially in difficult situations
- Impulse control – the ability to consider the impact of your behaviour and stop yourself doing something that is inappropriate

- Self-monitoring – the ability to reflect on your own behaviour and thoughts, both positively and critically, and to moderate your behaviour based on this self-analysis
- Planning and prioritisation of time – the ability to organise how you spend your time and understanding the urgency of specific tasks
- Organising – the ability to understand and arrange important tasks and information, and items needed to complete them
- Working memory – the ability to utilise information stored in your memory in such a way that it can help you to perform tasks
- Task initiation – the ability to begin a task and see it through to completion, without distraction

There is a widespread belief that children with ADHD lag 40 per cent behind their peers with executive-function skills, particularly those that focus on impulse and emotion control and self-moderation.[1] With this in mind, I hope you can see that punishing a child for what is effectively an immature level of executive functions is not only pointless, but potentially harmful to their self-esteem. They probably wish these skills were more developed, too, but they cannot change their brains. Again, the behaviour is not their fault, at least not at a conscious-choice level. As adults, we need to adjust our expectations of our children accordingly.

ADHD: a whistlestop neurophysiology and genetics tour

I'd like to close this chapter by taking you on a quick tour of the ADHD brain, and quite possibly the brains of those children with undiagnosed explosive behaviour, too. For me, understanding these neurological differences is key to really cementing the belief that 'it's not their fault'.

There is a strong neurobiological basis to ADHD. Brain scans have shown significant differences in specific receptors and transporters in the brain. Receptors are molecules that sit on the surface of each brain cell, their job being to pass chemical signals, a little like the postal-delivery system of the brain. Transporters are similar in role, except that they pass messages, or molecules, through the plasma membrane (a layer separating the inside and outside of a cell) – a little like the process of delivering a letter through a letterbox. One particular difference seen in the brain scans of children with ADHD compared to neurotypical children's is in the receptors and transporters of the neurotransmitter dopamine.[2] Many know dopamine as the 'feel-good hormone', but it isn't only involved in giving us pleasure and impacting mood – dopamine also plays a crucial role in our learning, attention and working memory, as well as movement control. A child with ADHD also displays differences in the density of the amygdalae and hippocampus (areas of the brain related to motivation and dopamine reward pathways).[3] Finally, MRI scans have shown several differences from a reduced total brain volume (3–4 per cent less in children with ADHD, compared to their neurotypical peers) to a reduction in grey matter in the areas of the brain related to attention and inhibition.[4]

There is a strong hereditary link with ADHD, with evidence suggesting that there may be genes passed on from generation to generation. Unfortunately, this field of research is relatively new and there is still much work to be done to understand specific genetic pathways. Studies of identical twins show us that ADHD has a high hereditary rate of around 74 per cent.[5] One study looking into the genetic links within families found a nine-fold increased likelihood of having ADHD in childhood if a sibling has it.[6] Perhaps the most convincing studies, however, when it comes to the genetics of ADHD, are those that involve looking at biological siblings who have been adopted into different families from birth. While critics of twin and sibling studies could argue that the research just indicates the impacts of parenting, environment or some sort of trauma experienced in the family (i.e. that ADHD is all down to nurture), adoption studies show that there is clearly a large link with biology, or the nature side of the nature/nurture argument. In these adoption studies, researchers have found that biological siblings adopted into different families at birth are more likely to have ADHD if their sibling does, than non-biological siblings within the adoptive family. In fact, adoptive siblings (i.e. those not biologically related) had no more increased risk of developing ADHD than a control group of unrelated children living in different homes.[7]

Unfortunately, scientists have yet to identify a specific 'ADHD gene', but reports of data, on over 20,000 individuals with ADHD and over 35,000 without, found that there were twelve different ADHD genetic risk variants.[8] It is possible, however, that rare variants will be discovered in the future. In 2023, researchers at Surrey University, UK, found a new gene that they believe is linked to the development of ADHD.[9] Danish researchers have recently identified twenty-seven specific loci on genes (a location on a chromosome where a gene is found – a little bit like a street number in a postal address), which are known to be related to ADHD that have alterations in individuals with ADHD.[10] Professor Ditte Demontis, at Denmark's Aarhus University, commented on the research findings saying: 'This emphasises that ADHD should be seen as a brain developmental disorder, and that it is most likely influenced by genes that have a major impact on the brain's early development.'

Perhaps one day we will have a genetic test, or even a targeted gene treatment therapy for ADHD. Until then, everyone, notably parents and carers, needs to understand that ADHD has a physiological basis. The brains of children with ADHD (and likely those with undiagnosed explosive behaviour) are not like those of their neurotypical peers, and expecting the same behaviour, or using the same behavioural techniques to try to control them, just isn't going to work. Most importantly, we must move away from the line of thinking that children with explosive behaviour are *choosing* to behave in this way. They didn't choose for their dopamine receptors to be different, they didn't choose for the loci on their genes to be altered, they didn't choose for their amygdalae to be less dense and they didn't choose for their executive-function skills to be less developed than their peers'. If the causes of ADHD and undiagnosed explosive behaviour are, indeed, largely physiological, this means that it is discriminatory to punish children for their condition and unethical to place blame on them for behaviour that is so often out of their control. *It simply isn't their fault.* And it also means that we should stop blaming ourselves (so much more on this in Chapter Nine) for something that is largely outside of our control.

We can't change our children, especially not those who are neurodivergent, but we can accept them for who they are and offer them support. As I pointed out earlier, it is when we stop trying to change them and meet them where they are that the magic happens.

I hope this chapter has helped you to understand your child's behaviour a little more. And now, we will carry the knowledge with us from this chapter to the next, as we move on to considering ways in which we can sometimes prevent difficult and explosive behaviour.

Chapter Four

Preventing explosive behaviour

M ost mainstream discipline techniques don't work. And especially when you have a child with ADHD or explosive behaviour.

I suspect this is something you have already discovered for yourself, but if you have sought behaviour advice from professionals, friends, family or even strangers on the internet, it's likely that you've been recommended the same old toolkit of punishments and rewards. Time out, the naughty step, ignoring the bad behaviour and praising the good, sticker charts, marbles in a jar or various consequences, ranging from taking away a fun activity to removing freedom (something often known as 'grounding') are among the techniques most commonly recommended for tackling challenging behaviour. I remember stumbling upon an online discussion group for parents of children with ADHD and being horrified at how outdated, authoritarian and harsh the discipline advice was.

We are obsessed with controlling and coercing children, ruling them through fear and demanding respect, and I have spoken often about childism in my work – the discrimination and poor treatment of children by adults in society. When those children have ADHD, the control and fear-based discipline ramp up a gear. Only none of it works. I know it, you know it, our children know it. I wonder if the people recommending it also know it – they just don't know what else to do. It reminds me of the famous saying 'Insanity is doing the same thing over and over again and expecting different results' (often attributed to Albert Einstein, albeit likely incorrectly). When we constantly punish or try to bribe children with ADHD or undiagnosed explosive behaviour, we are not only wasting our time and energy, but also likely making things worse. Do you remember the cycle of shame in the previous chapter, where the child's poor behaviour leads to shaming and punishment, causing them to feel useless and more dysregulated, making their behaviour even worse? The key to not only surviving, but thriving when you are raising or, indeed, teaching a child with ADHD or explosive behaviour is to completely rethink everything you have been taught and already tried before.

Introducing the 'behaviour tree'

Whenever I work with parents or carers who are struggling with a child's behaviour, I always explain that they need to leave behind simplistic and quick-fix discipline approaches that suggest all they need to do is to utter some magic words or emulate the techniques of a TV parenting show or a social media video. There is no such thing as an easy solution, especially one that doesn't even skim the surface of what's actually happening for the child.

My approach is three-pronged, and while it may not be a magic solution that works in mere hours or days, it doesn't just temporarily mask or palliate, but makes real, lasting change. Perhaps you are aware of the Greek symbol Ψ (psi), often used to represent the word psychology? Or perhaps you recognise it as the trident of Poseidon, Greek god of the sea? Keep that symbol, or shape, in your mind and imagine it as a tree. The central vertical line (or the handle of the trident) is the trunk of the tree, and the left and right arms are the branches.

You and your relationship with your child are the trunk of the behaviour tree. This is the core of everything, the tree roots run deep and provide the support and structure for the tree to grow and bloom, providing nutrients and nurturance. The trunk is by far the most important section. You cannot attempt to change your child's behaviour unless you have a strong trunk and roots. Everything starts with you.

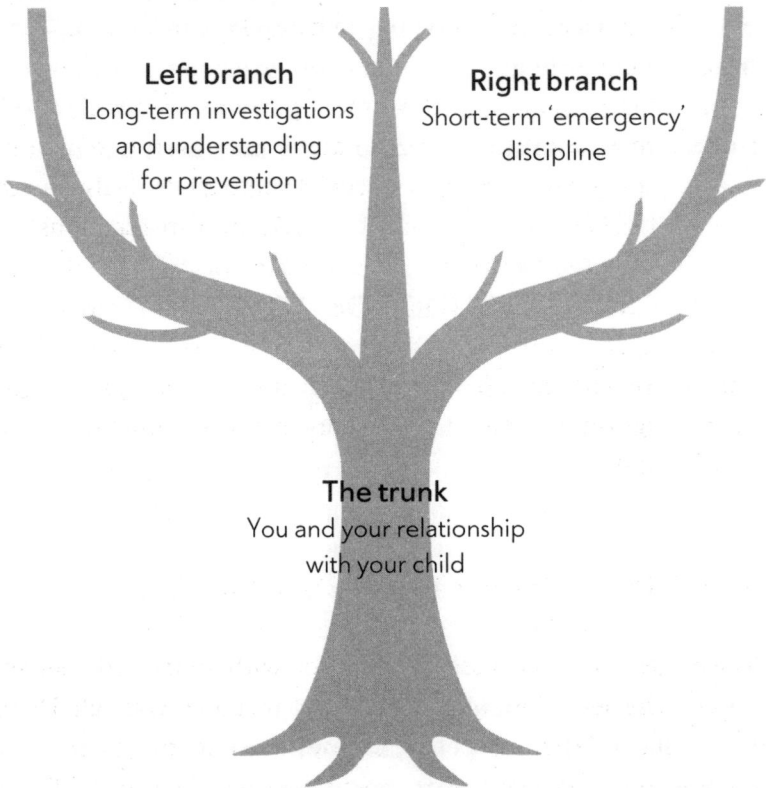

Left branch
Long-term investigations
and understanding
for prevention

Right branch
Short-term 'emergency'
discipline

The trunk
You and your relationship
with your child

The left-hand branch represents understanding your child, their triggers, any hurdles that they face, any unmet needs they may have and the impact on them of different environments. This branch is about you playing detective to prevent as much tricky behaviour as possible and having a long-term view and goals of your child's behaviour.

The right-hand branch represents safety – for your child, others and yourself – and dealing with difficult and explosive behaviour in the moment. It's what I term 'emergency discipline'. This section is about what to do when your detective work and your support and role modelling aren't quite enough and your child explodes into out-of-control and potentially dangerous behaviour. It's not just about what you do in the short term to make things easier for everybody, but also how to 'clean up' and heal after explosions.

Most common discipline techniques in our society only think short term or consider the right-hand branch of the behaviour tree. But for an effective and respectful approach to dealing with your child's behaviour, you must consider all three sections.

In this chapter I'd like to focus on the trunk and the left-hand branch of the tree – you, your relationship with your child, their needs, triggers and your understanding of them. In the next chapter we will pick up on this idea again, but with a sole focus on the right-hand branch, or 'emergency discipline' during a behavioural crisis.

The tree trunk – the part you play

The biggest tool you possess to help you with your child's behaviour (or the behaviour of children in your care) is yourself. Here, I don't mean learning specific phrases to recite to your child or memorising role-play scenarios you have watched on TikTok. I mean something far deeper and more effective. The way you act, feel and regulate your own behaviour around your child will have the biggest impact on how they are able to regulate theirs. All children look to the adults in their lives to learn how to behave; neurodivergent children are no different.

The tricky thing here is that children with ADHD or un-diagnosed explosive behaviour are far more likely to be on the receiving end of harsh discipline, disconnect, shaming and blaming than their neurotypical peers. Please don't think I am blaming *you* for anything here. I know how hard it is to raise a child with ADHD and explosive behaviour. I know how hard it is to be neurodivergent yourself. And I know how hard it is to stay calm and nurturing when you don't have any support and others look at you as if you are the problem. I also know that most discipline advice for parents and carers of children with ADHD and explosive behaviour centres on the adult being 'in charge', 'letting them know who's boss', 'not letting them get away with anything' and 'staying in control'. These messages seep slowly into your subconscious and, even though in your heart you feel a more nurturing approach is probably best for your family, the authoritarian naysayers make you second-guess everything. Add to this the stigma and the pressure of attempting to keep your cool while trying to get anything done and it's hard to be the example that you want to set for your child.

I'm not saying you need to be perfect. Far from it (again, Chapter Ten covers this in detail). But what I am saying is that it's time to trust your instincts to follow a kinder path with your child and shut out any noise from those who say otherwise.

The three most important elements of our tree trunk all happen to start with a C. They are co-regulation, containment and collaboration. Let's look at each of these in turn.

Co-regulation

Before self-regulation comes co-regulation. It is key to helping children with ADHD and explosive behaviour manage their emotions.

Co-regulation is a term used in psychology to describe someone's ability to regulate their emotions with the help of somebody else. This doesn't just apply to parents and children; it applies to everybody. For instance, if you were upset and your best friend gave you a hug, it may help you to feel a bit better; or if you are scared about something, your partner talking it through with you might help you to feel a bit calmer. The person who is helping you to regulate may not be able to assist with solving any underlying problems but spending time with them allows you to feel better about the problems and more able to tackle them alone. Similarly, they may not be able to help you to reach a complete state of calmness, but they can help to take the edge off.

In order for co-regulation to work well, one party needs to be regulated and calm, so that they can share a sense of safety and security. This is usually the role that parents and carers play in an adult–child relationship. Some of us did not learn the skill of co-regulation from our own parents when we were children, instead being sent away to our rooms when we were dysregulated and behaving 'poorly', or constantly shamed or bribed into behaving 'better', or sometimes being on the receiving end of even more dysregulation if our parents yelled at or hit us. If this reflects your own upbringing (as it does, unfortunately, for many) and co-regulation is a new concept to you, it can be harder to embrace it. But it's never too late to learn.

If your child's behaviour is out of control and they are struggling to manage their emotions, stepping in with calmness and sharing with them your ability to regulate (or co-regulating) is the most powerful thing you can do to prevent the behaviour escalating, and also to teach them the skills they need to help with self-regulation in the future.

How can we learn to be better at co-regulation as parents or carers?

First, we need to consider our own thoughts and feelings, working through any issues that are holding us back from being calmer. If we bring our own problems to tricky interactions with our children, we not only prevent co-regulation, but we can make their behaviour much worse. This is about looking into our own lives – trying to offload as many things as possible that may make us feel scared, stressed, angry, frustrated and out of control, finding help with those that we can't (therapy is a great form of co-regulation) and adding in more things that bring us peace and joy (much more on this in Chapter Ten).

Next, we need to focus on our patience and ability to 'hold' our children's difficult emotions, rather than feeling the urge to sweep in and fix everything quickly because we feel uncomfortable. Children cry, they get angry, they have big emotions – and this is all OK. But for many of us who weren't on the receiving end of co-regulation as children we can struggle with the ability to be around a child who is sad, angry or scared. The simplest first step here is to acknowledge that it is normal for children to have these emotions, and while they need our support to work through them, they don't need us to sweep them away instantly.

Expectations of your child's behaviour and their ability to regulate their emotions play a big role, too. This is why I spent so long in the previous chapter explaining why explosive, out-of-control behaviour is not your child's fault. When we truly understand ADHD and the roots of explosive behaviour, we can approach children through the lens of their struggles. And when we see them in this light, our immediate response is one of wanting to help them, with co-regulation, rather than hurting them, with punishment, shaming or sending them away from us.

Finally, we have to focus on patience – not just with our children, but with ourselves, too, particularly if co-regulation is a new skill. It is absolutely something that we can all learn to do, but it's going to take time. We are not going to be pros as soon as we start. There are going to be times when we just don't have anything left in us after a tough day, times when we may make things worse and times when we try, but don't quite manage to see things through until a point when our child becomes more regulated. Sometimes we may absorb our child's dysregulation, helping them in the moment, but feeling worse ourselves afterwards. This is all normal and will improve over time. The more we practise, the better our co-regulation skills will get.

Please don't beat yourself up for any failed attempts. The fact that you have even tried is a good sign and so much better than so many other adults when they are around explosive and out-of-control behaviour from children. If you keep trying, you will get better.

Containment

Containment is a crucial part of co-regulation. It is the ability of the adult to 'hold' a child's big feelings and protect them from emotional and physical harm. The parent or carer acts as a container (like a metaphorical Tupperware) to allow the child to offload feelings and emotions that are too difficult for them to hold on to alone. As adults, it is our capacity to hold these feelings in our own larger, more mature containers and transform them into something safer, less harmful and less stressful for our children that allows them to reach a state of regulation. Of course, if our containers are full up and we are unable to clip the lid on, then the minute our child starts overflowing, we are unable to contain their emotions and may add to the problem with our own explosion. I'm sure you know what I mean here. I think all parents, especially those of children with explosive behaviour, have experienced a time when their own behaviour has been more alarming than that of their child. I have reached this point a couple of times over the last two decades, and my behaviour has actually scared me (I'll tell you more about one particular example in Chapter Ten). This is not a time to berate yourself, but it is indicative of the need for a deep level of self-acceptance and self-nurturance and an understanding that you desperately need to make space in your own container.

Collaboration

Moving away from discipline through coercion and control (which sums up almost all popular forms of behaviour management used today, both at home and at school) to an approach that is rooted in collaboration is the most effective style for all children, but especially those with ADHD or undiagnosed explosive behaviour. Collaboration is all about working together to identify and solve problems. Tricky behaviour and situations are approached as a team; it's you and your child versus the issue, rather than you positioning yourself against your child in a battle, with an unfair balance of power tipped in your favour.

Collaboration gives children a voice, rather than demanding silent obedience. It gives them choices, rather than demands. It treats them with respect, as people, right from the beginning of life, rather than somehow only gaining respect as adults. In a world full of stigma and adversity faced by children with behavioural challenges, collaboration says 'I love you; I see you, I'm here for you'. It teaches children that they can trust you. And when they can trust that you will always be on their side, even when they've done something wrong, they are more likely to come to you and ask for your help or tell you when they've done something wrong and ask for assistance with fixing it. Collaboration isn't a magic tool (nothing is), and your child's behaviour will still be all over the place, because that's the nature of their ADHD or the undiagnosed issues underlying their behaviour (more on this in a bit) – but when children and their parents or carers work together as a team, great things can happen.

What does this collaboration look like in reality? It means giving your child a voice as much as possible – for instance, discussing how to overcome specific situations that they find hard and listening to their suggestions, asking for their input on any family rules or boundaries, encouraging them to add their point of view to any discussions surrounding their behaviour or actions and giving them agency and autonomy over their life whenever you can.

It's never too early to start with a collaborative approach, even if your child is much younger and this verbal communication is developmentally out of their reach. At its core, this is about fostering mutual respect and empathy, and while your child may not be able to hold a full-on conversation with you yet, you can still allow them as much autonomy over their life as possible, through their eating (when, how much and what they eat), their play (what, where, when and how they play, and who plays with them) and their everyday interactions with you (for instance, how toothbrushing happens, choosing their clothing in the morning and how and when they bathe).

Collaboration helps children to feel valued, which can help with their self-esteem (moving them out of the cycle of shame), their relationship with you (which can help with co-regulation) and their trust in you (which makes them more likely to ask you for help when they're struggling). From your point of view, it feels so much nicer to have a positive relationship with your child, working together as a team, than a combative one, with constant fighting. Collaboration is good for everybody.

The magic really happens when co-regulation, containment and collaboration are combined. Does it mean your child's behaviour will suddenly become 'easy' and calm? Absolutely not. But it does mean that your child will stand the best chance of developing self-regulation skills and a structure to support their emotions as they grow. It also alters your relationship to a more positive, empathetic, nurturing and fulfilling one, and when you feel better about your child and your relationship with them, you are better at co-regulating and containing, in an ever-increasing circle of positivity and far-reaching effects.

The three Cs take practice. You won't nail them all immediately, and you will still slip up and make mistakes, but shifting from a punitive, coercive, controlling mindset to a supportive and understanding one is the key to growing the roots of your behaviour tree as deep as possible and its trunk as sturdy as can be.

The left-hand tree branch: understanding and preventing explosive behaviour

I often hear parents complaining that 'gentle parenting' (the style of parenting I am known for – one rooted in respect, understanding and empathy for children) 'doesn't work'. When I ask them to clarify what they mean, they reel off a long list of things they have tried with their child and which have had no impact on their behaviour, usually comprised of what I call 'firefighting' or tackling difficult behaviour as it happens. These parents spend most of their time trying to put out fires of out-of-control and explosive behaviour and they are exhausted when they keep reigniting. While they may handle the behaviour well in the moment, what they usually miss is a consideration of its triggers. Uncovering the underlying cause so that they can work to prevent the behaviour in the first place is what will bring about the biggest change. As the saying goes, 'prevention is better than cure', and while you won't be able to prevent all explosive behaviour (or probably even half of it), investing time and energy into understanding your child's triggers is time well spent indeed.

The explosive volcano

I was fortunate enough to spend some time on the island of Sicily with my family recently, staying very close to Mount Etna, the active volcano. My eldest child is a geologist and he had put us all at ease about our proximity to the volcano in the weeks running up to our holiday. Once we arrived, however, Mama Etna (as she is known locally) was going through a period of heightened activity, with regular firework-like eruptions that we could witness from our accommodation, accompanied by loud, bone-shaking booms. We would often wake to find a layer of volcanic ash covering everything. The first time this happened, we were excited to have witnessed such as spectacle of nature; when it continued, however, we became a little apprehensive, to say the least. My son took the opportunity for some co-regulation, as he gave us all a quick volcanology lesson, some of which I'd like to share with you (bear with me, there is a reason for this!).

I have to begin with a quick apology to any geologists who are reading, as I am sure I have butchered some of my son's explanations and, to this end, he has asked me to add a disclaimer here, noting that these are my words and not his. But I think the explanation I'm about to give is a great analogy to help us understand explosive behaviour in children and the best way to approach it as an adult caring for them.

When certain types of volcanoes like Etna erupt, they do so because molten rock, known as magma, pushes up through the crust of the earth. The pressure of the magma builds under the volcano until the point that it explodes. During this process, gases trapped within the magma are released into the atmosphere. Regular gas release, known as degassing, helps to reduce the explosiveness of any eruptions. Think of the process as a little like having a bottle of Coke (other fizzy drinks brands are available!) that has been shaken up. Degassing here is akin to slowly and carefully untwisting the cap to release some of the gas, instead of letting the pressure build so much that the cap is blown off all at once, followed by a swift explosion of Coke everywhere. The fact that Mama Etna was regularly degassing, accompanied by some little spurts of magma and some rather loud burps may have looked alarming to us non-geologists, but to those in the know it was a positive sign that a dangerous and massive eruption was unlikely.

The concept of degassing makes me think of ADHD, and how it's better for us, as adults, to be a safe space to allow our child to regularly offload their dysregulated emotions, rather than forcing them to mask and keep it all in, resulting in a major, potentially dangerous explosion. Our co-regulation and containment act as the degassing. While we may wish for no difficult behaviour at all, this isn't realistic and, most importantly, if we cannot support our children when they are dysregulated with us, they are going to be far worse when they are away from us.

EXERCISE: FINDING YOUR CHILD'S MAGMA AND VOLCANIC GASES

If we view the molten magma of a volcano as a trigger for our child's dysregulation, then we can view the gases as resulting dysregulated emotions and the degassing as early-warning signs that a major eruption may happen if we don't step in with some containment and co-regulation.

Using the illustration below, try to add some notes to help you make an early identification of warning signs and underlying triggers that a potential explosion is incoming. I have added some ideas to get you started, but feel free to cross them out if they don't apply to your child, as well as adding your own.

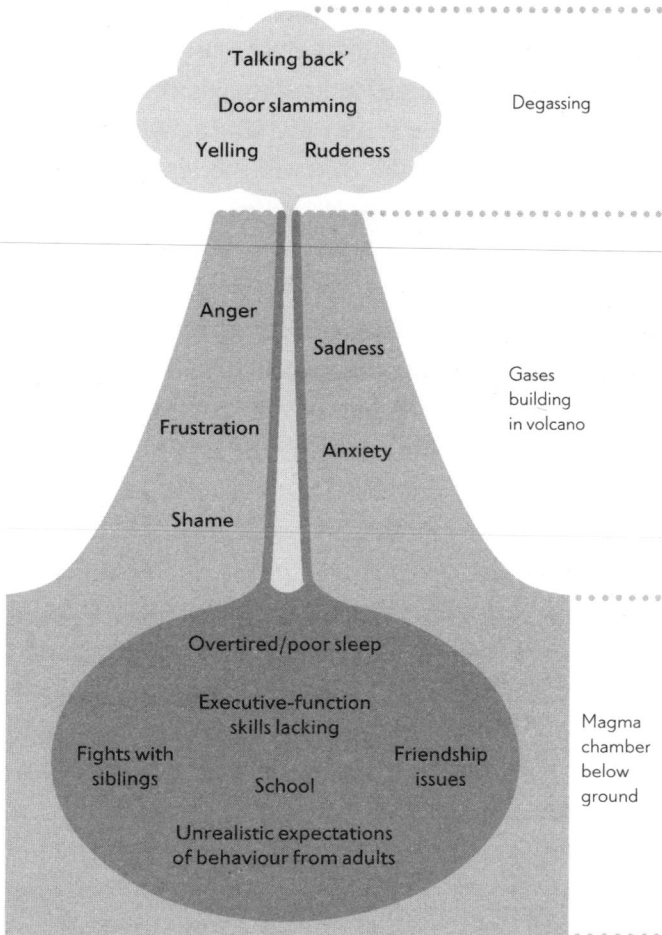

'Talking back'

Door slamming

Degassing

Yelling   Rudeness

Anger

Sadness

Gases
building
in volcano

Frustration

Anxiety

Shame

Overtired/poor sleep

Executive-function
skills lacking

Fights with
siblings

Friendship
issues

Magma
chamber
below
ground

School

Unrealistic expectations
of behaviour from adults

A quick note on implosive behaviour

Although the focus on this book is the explosive behaviour that often accompanies ADHD, or exists without an ADHD diagnosis, I think it's important to revisit the idea that ADHD doesn't necessarily always result in explosive behaviour, particularly not in girls. We have already discussed that for many, the hyperactivity may be internal, with a whizzing and buzzing brain; similarly, not all dysregulated emotions explode outwardly – some implode instead. These internalised emotions may initially seem easier for parents and carers to manage; however, they can be far more damaging because they are all directed at the person who is already struggling and who will therefore suffer the most damage: the child themselves. Here, I'm talking about anxiety, depression and negative self-talk, and potentially developing self-harming behaviours.

Implosive behaviours often share the same triggers. Using the analogy of the volcano, the magma chamber is often full of the same underlying problems, and the resulting dysregulated emotions are analogous to those gases sitting just below the surface. However, 'de-gassing' doesn't occur; instead, everything gets sucked back into the volcano like some sort of black hole. My geologist son did try to explain the physics of black holes to me to help with this section, but my (suspected) inattentive ADHD brain could not listen for more than a few seconds before spacing out, so I'm afraid here is where my metaphor ends. Just know that implosive behaviour is equally in need of co-regulation and containment as explosive, if not more so. Quiet children are not always the parenting prize that society so desires.

Building self-esteem

'Sit still!' 'Stop moving.' 'Stop being disruptive.' 'Don't be an idiot.' 'Pay attention!' 'Behave!' 'You're not trying hard enough.' 'You're stupid.' 'You're so immature.' 'You're so difficult.' 'Why can't you be more like your sister?' 'You're always causing trouble.' 'You should be ashamed of yourself.' 'Why can't you be normal?'

Can you imagine a life growing up hearing things such as this every day? Or perhaps you don't have to imagine too hard if you have lived experience. Experts estimate that children with ADHD have received 20,000 more negative messages by the age of ten than their neurotypical peers.[1] The impact of this near-constant criticism and character assassination on children's self-esteem and confidence can be devastating. And if we add rejection sensitive dysphoria (RSD) to the picture, which, if you remember, is a common co-existing condition for those with ADHD (see page 32), the added sensitivity can hit a child with ADHD with a double blow to their confidence. It's no wonder that so many children end up in the cycle of shame, their self-esteem tanking as their explosive behaviour escalates.

The role of adults here is simple: we need to rebuild the self-esteem of these children. The more explosive (or implosive) the behaviour, the more we need to fill their minds and hearts with love, assurance, hopefulness and positivity. We need to tell them what we love about them, what makes them special, how good they make us feel, how they make us laugh and how we appreciate them for who they are. We need to be their champions and their cheerleaders. We need to recognise their talents, their skills and their hard work and tell them how proud we are – and do all this more than we point out their flaws or their mistakes.

We do have to be careful here, however, to not place too much pressure on them. We need to let them know that it's OK to make mistakes, that everybody is human, including us. We need to read their emotions and not go so far the other way that they prefer not to try something for fear of failing. Sadly, this is a very real and common pattern displayed by children with ADHD, who become risk averse, not just to avoid punishment, but also to avoid not receiving a reward if their attempts are not good enough.

Research has shown that children with ADHD are more likely than neurotypical children to abandon a task if they feel they will lose a promised reward.[2] This risk aversion is often a protection mechanism for children who are so used to failure, but it does highlight how careful parents and carers need to be with their balance of offering praise and rewards, which can very quickly end up denting self-esteem and effort if children don't receive them or give up because they fear failure.

How else can you help to increase your child's self-esteem? Let's take a quick look at some ideas.

Teach your child about ADHD

The chances are that your child has had pressure to change their behaviour placed on them by many adults, including yourself, other family members and teaching staff, if they are at school. Perhaps your child has desperately tried to change, to avoid punishment or to gain rewards, but they just couldn't produce the behaviour that was desired or expected of them.

I'm sure you can see how this can quickly cause them to believe that they are the problem, and that they are not good enough when they fail to produce the desired behaviour change. The saddest thing is that children with ADHD so often blame themselves for their behaviour and this damages their self-esteem. The solution here is simple: to teach them about ADHD. Once they understand that their brains are wired differently to others' – and that this likely affects their ability to concentrate, control their impulses and their emotions, sit still, be quiet, organise themselves and remember things – all that pressure and shame are lifted. There are no right or wrong ways to teach your child about ADHD, and there are some great books available to help kickstart conversations (see Resources, page 223) and invite questions. And if you are neurodivergent yourself, you can discuss your own experiences with your child, too.

Teach them to not aim for perfection

Perfectionism is common in children with ADHD, particularly girls. This can cause children to freeze because of fear of failure. Often, their worry about not achieving perfection can be so overwhelming that they would prefer to not even try. It is easier for them to accept the frustration of others if they refuse to do something than it is to achieve less than perfect if they do give something a go. This is also partly why I am so anti the idea of ADHD being a superpower; it places extra pressure on children, sending the message that they have to be 'extra' and achieve more than neurotypical children – to be 'super' when they are just trying to get through the day. As adults, we need to help children to understand that not everything is easy and that's OK.

You probably won't be surprised to learn that teaching your child to overcome perfectionism starts with you. Maybe you have the trait yourself (especially if you have ADHD)? If so, letting your child see you try and fail to achieve something, while being proud of yourself for giving it a go, is so important. Modelling self-acceptance yourself is powerful, showing that it is OK to accept your failures. Failures mean that we are learning and growing and, importantly, trying. Be careful to not focus too much verbal praise on your child's achievements, too. While it may feel like a way to raise their self-esteem, placing a focus on times when they excel sets a bar that they feel they need to constantly hit. Instead, try to focus most of your praise on their attempts, no matter the outcome.

Find something that they enjoy

Friendships and social settings can often be hard for children with ADHD and explosive behaviour. Parents of other children (or the children themselves) may not want them to spend time with yours, incorrectly viewing them as 'a bad influence', and playdates and party invites can be thin on the ground. Finding a social activity where they feel included and valued is so important, and a place where they can pursue their interests and feel good about themselves and be authentic can be a huge confidence booster.

We tried many different clubs and classes when Flynn was younger and most of them didn't stick for various reasons, mostly involving his ADHD traits. But we did find a club that felt like home. For us it was Boys' Brigade, a little like the Cubs and Scouts movement. Our local Boys' Brigade was run by amazing, nurturing volunteers who had so much patience; in fact, I think the staff, rather than the group or even the activity, make all the difference. They accommodated Flynn's needs, and he was never made to feel like a problem. He started attending once a week when he was five years old and didn't leave until he was eighteen. In those thirteen years, he took part in so many amazing activities, from camping holidays to karting, archery, walking competitions and achieving badges and awards. He even attained the highest award the Boys' Brigade offer: the King's Badge, which involved learning new skills, attending residential training and a period of volunteering. Seeing the pride on Flynn's face when he received his King's Badge award, shortly before he turned eighteen, was a perfect end to his time at Boys'

Brigade. The change this weekly meet made to his self-esteem over the years was obvious, and I am so thankful he had the opportunity. I am certain that somewhere there is an equally confidence-boosting activity awaiting your child.

Help them to find a village

While teaching children about ADHD is a great starting point, meeting with other neurodivergent children, and hopefully finding their tribe, is key to them feeling truly understood and accepted. In a world where they spend most of their time trying to fit into a neurotypical world, full of neurotypical children, having a community where they don't need to mask and won't be misunderstood is the ultimate way to boost their self-esteem. If your child is younger, then you meeting other parents, and being able to sit down with them and chat about your similar experiences is really confidence boosting for you, too.

If your child is older, or you cannot find a 'village' local to you, joining internet discussion groups and online meet-ups comes a close second for increasing self-esteem. Do be careful of internet safety if your child will have unsupervised access, though. Not everybody is who they seem to be, and no area of the internet is truly safe, especially for children who may struggle with their executive functions, including impulsivity and really thinking through the repercussions of something before they say or do it.

Create an environment for them to succeed

Too often we place so much pressure on children with 'difficult behaviour' to change, when what we really need to change is the world to fit our children. What I'm saying here is that if anybody in your child's life needs to make changes, it is the adults, including you. Shift the onus of change away from your child and instead think about adjustments that you can make, perhaps practical, or in your expectations, which will make life easier for them. Here are some examples:

- If visiting a certain place always causes problems, do you really need to go there? (Or can you go without your child?)
- If doing something at a certain time is problematic, perhaps because your child is tired, or hungry or overwhelmed after a long day, is it possible for you to go alone? Or at a different time?
- If your child finds a certain task difficult, what can you change to make it easier for them? For instance, if mornings before school are difficult and they become overwhelmed with trying to find everything they need, could you help them to get everything ready the night before? Or if they're older, help them to produce a to-do list that they can pin on the back of their bedroom door?
- If your child always struggles to remember their homework, could you ask their teacher to make a note for them in their homework diary at the end of the lesson?
- If your child will be doing something new, make sure they know what will happen, where they are going and what they will be doing in advance. Even better, can you utilise photos, virtual walk-throughs and role play, and encourage questions from them. Preparation is key for children with ADHD and explosive (or implosive) behaviour.
- Embrace visual guides, such as chore charts and timetables, which can help children to feel more in

control of everyday activities. They also act as good memory joggers, aiding their developing working-memory skills.

- If your child struggles to sit still in a group or class, would it be possible for them to sit on a wobble cushion (a round, inflatable cushion that provides small movements, wobbling to encourage the child to move slightly to keep their balance) or a swivel seat pad (this sits on the chair, allowing them to twist from side to side), use chair bands (thick elastic bands that fix around the chair legs, allowing them to move their feet in a way that is not noisy or disruptive) or even try a standing desk at the back of the room, enabling them to move around or pace while they work, or listen.
- Look into fiddle and fidget toys. There are so many different ones on the market today that suit every sensory need and they can help children to feel more regulated. Although many view them as tools for use in an educational setting, they can be used anywhere, including at home.

Don't be afraid to ask for places and people to accommodate your child. As I mentioned previously, the world is designed for neurotypical children, but a few small tweaks and tools can make a huge difference to children who would otherwise be restless in an environment not geared to their needs.

Be and provide a safe haven

Before I end this chapter with some personal accounts from my son and other parents, I'd like to revisit the idea of containment, co-regulation and degassing. We discussed earlier how important it is for parents of children with ADHD and undiagnosed explosive behaviour to stay as calm and supportive as possible, enabling them to be authentic at home, and to spend time in an environment where they can experience co-regulation. When children feel safe with us, we can expect regular degassing. As adults, we must understand that this is a good thing (although we would probably rather our children were 'well behaved' with us) and that giving them the opportunity to regularly degas in our company, or in their own space in the safety and security of home, is the ultimate way to prevent as many huge eruptions as possible.

I guess what I'm really saying here is don't sweat the small stuff. Don't be tempted to pick your child up on every rude comment, every toy they don't put away, every door they slam or piece of rubbish they don't put in the bin. You don't have to always uphold every boundary, and you don't have to discipline every little misdemeanour. The next time your child does something that triggers you, ask yourself, *Are they degassing? Will it be better in the long run if I let this go?* Allowing them this grace is not only less stressful for them, but for you, too.

I asked my son Flynn what he thought I could have done better as a parent to help him when he felt his behaviour was getting out of control, or if he could give any advice to parents of children with explosive behaviour. Here's what he told me:

> *Don't shout at them. If I was shouted at, I would just shout back. You need the adult to be calm. Also, don't lecture. When I was poorly behaved, I knew it was wrong and that I should stop, but I literally couldn't stop. Be patient. If you ask them to do something and they don't do it straight away, just wait; if they're like me, they will do it eventually, but constantly asking or nagging doesn't help. For instance, if I was meant to be tidying my room, I would try to start but then I'd*

find something else, completely irrelevant, and get stuck in that. I would find a box full of old things and then spend ages looking through it, then realise my room wasn't done. Rather than telling me off for not tidying, it would have helped if you had just checked in on me every now and again in a happy and nice way.

Watching videos and gaming helps me to feel calm. But ADHD comes with hyper-fixation and games were my fixation, so that's both good and bad, I guess. But screen time really does help. As I've got older, I game less, and don't get so fixated.

I think you have to accept the child. Other than really understanding and being patient, there's not much more that you can do. Rather than trying to change the child, understanding them, and accepting them is the best way. I find a lot of people don't really understand ADHD, and I've had to spend a lot of time explaining it to people. When they have knowledge, then they're supportive, but it's hard because there are so many misconceptions about it.

I also spoke with some parents of children with ADHD and asked them what they found to be the most helpful things to do during times of heightened stress and difficult behaviour, or ways that they had found to reduce the difficult times. Here's what they told me:

'Lots of empathy and validation is important for my child, as like so many ADHD children he can have a very heightened sense of shame, but I have to get the balance right, because too much talking about emotions can cause him to get very "stuck" and unable to move forward. It also can lead him to look for negatives at times, as he learned that that elicited a lot of attention from me in the past – I am trying to shift the way that I give attention to things, so that he knows he can get attention from me without something having to be "wrong".'

'My son's outbursts can sometimes seem to be triggered by very little, although I think of him as a bit of a Coke bottle. Always fizzing under the surface. Over the last three years, I have been given all kinds of advice from reward charts to distractions. I didn't get anywhere with any of them. Distraction doesn't work, as when he is angry, he becomes very focused on causing maximum damage and he lacks the ability to rationalise in those moments. The difficult part of all of this for me has been coping with him trying to hurt me while maintaining our close relationship. It is very hard at times to remain patient and calm, but nothing good comes out of becoming dysregulated myself.'

'I think my daughter is really triggered by a lack of self-esteem. I can see her pulling away from us and her friends when she's feeling down. If I can catch it early, a big cuddle and a chat often helps, but if I miss it when she's sinking, then it's almost inevitable that she will have a big emotional explosion.'

'I've realised that my son uses me and his dad as a sort of emotional punchbag. It took me a long time to see it and, at first, I would punish him for being rude, but now I know if he's had a bad day at school or with his friends because he will come home in a strop. Instead of sending him to his room and banning him from his Xbox, I let him know that I'm there for him if he needs me and take him a drink and a packet of crisps to help him to decompress. I try not to take anything rude he says too personally because I know it's not really about me; it's just that he feels safe to let it out with me, which I'd rather he did than let it out on his siblings or at school.'

'As my daughter has got older, I've got better at pinpointing her triggers. For her, a lack of sleep and hunger are big ones, and also if there is change to her normal routines. I try to stick to normal as much as possible, especially during the summer holidays, and I've set up a little snack station that she has free access to. It doesn't stop all the meltdowns, but it definitely helps.'

There are, sadly, no shortcuts when it comes to parenting. As much as we may wish we have a magic wand, or a phrase with mystical obedience powers, there is no such thing. After two decades of raising a child with ADHD and explosive behaviour, and working with other parents, I have come to the conclusion that it is far easier to change ourselves than to make constant (usually failed) attempts to change them.

To return to our tree: here, the main focus is on the strong roots and trunk, or our ability to help our children to co-regulate, to contain their big emotions and collaborate with them, working as a team. Alongside this focus on our own behaviour, if we concentrate on the first (left) branch of the tree, where we play detective and try to uncover and remove as many triggers as possible, we will be in the best position to help our children, to raise their self-esteem and take the edge off any tricky behaviour.

What happens if an eruption is looming or actually happens? That's exactly what we'll cover in the next chapter, as we talk about the remaining branch of the tree: coping in the moment and keeping everybody safe.

Chapter Five

How to cope when your child's behaviour is out of control

When you have a baby, you are inundated with advice on how to bathe, feed and help them sleep at night. But I've always thought a portion of antenatal classes should be dedicated to understanding behaviour as they grow and things start to get a little more complicated. Yes, babies are hard work, you are exhausted from living on little sleep, but their needs are also quite simple. If they cry, most are usually settled with a breast or bottle, a hug and some rocking. As children get older, though, their behaviour not only becomes more perplexing, but it also becomes harder to cope with when you can't solve everything with a quick milk feed. When that little baby who would lie so snuggly in your arms grows to half your size (or bigger) and cannot be placated as easily, that's when I think the really tough element of parenting kicks in. If your child's behaviour is often out of control, you can feel like a novice parent all over again. I remember the feelings of hopelessness I experienced often, wishing for the days when I understood my son's behaviour and could sweep in and make everything OK again in seconds, or minutes.

Sometimes, despite all the best preparation and detective work, there are times when you simply cannot prevent explosions and meltdowns. When they happen, it doesn't mean that you have somehow failed as a parent, and neither does it mean that your child is choosing to act this way deliberately, to wind you up or to annoy staff, if it happens in daycare or at school. Explosions happen when the degassing we learned about in the previous chapter doesn't reduce the pressure your child is experiencing and usually one final thing, often small, is enough to send fiery lava soaring up into the sky, leaving a trail of devastation behind it. Again, this is not your fault, and neither is it the fault of your child; what you do during this time, however, is crucial – not only to keep yourself, your child and everybody else safe, but also to try to protect their self-esteem as much as possible.

Why punishment doesn't work

There is a pervasive view in our society that when children 'act up', they should be 'taught a lesson'. Or, in other words, when their behaviour is unacceptable, we should punish them so that they will not choose to behave so poorly in the future. That punishment should be commensurate with the intensity of their behaviour and the scale of their misdemeanour. If they have done something relatively small and inconsequential, a stern telling off or sending them to their room should, supposedly, suffice. If the behaviour is out of control and has resulted in something being broken, somebody being hurt or rules being breached, then the presumption here is that the punishment should be more severe. Taking away privileges – access to screens, socialising, free time, money and beloved toys – often tops the list of recommended punishments, although some believe in scaring (through yelling, or perhaps physical punishment) and shaming (by making them publicly apologise, or worse, sharing details of their 'crime' on social media). The idea here is that the more fear or embarrassment the child feels, the less likely they are to behave in similarly 'antisocial' ways in the future.

At first, this seems like a sensible idea. After all, this is how most of society operates. If you break a law, you will be fined or imprisoned. If you do something terrible at work, you will be fired. Proponents of the 'tough-love' approach liken it to preparing children for 'the real world'. These same people complain that the problem with 'the kids of today' is that 'parents wrap them up in cotton wool and want to be their friends'. They will spend ages reminiscing about the good old days of the cane, spanking, being sent to bed with no dinner or having their mouths washed out with soap, in the same misty-eyed way that some elderly people remember living through a world war. The trouble is punishment doesn't work. It doesn't work for neurotypical children, and it certainly doesn't work for those with ADHD.

The thinking behind the behaviourist idea that if you make a child feel bad enough, they won't repeat the behaviour is the misguided viewpoint that the child has always been, and will be in the future, in control of their behaviour. If a child is meant to consider their actions and decide on a plan that is more socially acceptable, the underlying principle here is that they are always able to regulate their emotions and have conscious control over their actions. But this isn't true. As adults, with fully mature brains, we will often struggle to do this. So why do we expect our children to be better than us? We know that children with ADHD have underdeveloped executive-function skills, we know that their brains develop differently and areas that are responsible for impulse control and emotion regulation do not operate in the same way as their neurotypical peers' (and even then, a neurotypical child does not have the same control over their behaviour as a neurotypical adult). Expecting them to be able to turn on a switch at will to be fully in control of their behaviour is ridiculously naïve. The sad reality, then, is that not only does punishment simply not work, but for children with ADHD or undiagnosed explosive behaviour it can make things much, much worse.

Is there a place for rewards?

Once you realise how utterly pointless punishments are for explosive behaviour, naturally thoughts turn to rewards. Everybody likes a reward, don't they? Rewards make people feel good. This is true, sometimes. But in the previous chapter we discussed how overly praising or rewarding a child with ADHD for their behaviour and actions can actually undermine their self-esteem and confidence, add to their perfectionism and cause them to procrastinate, or simply not try, through fear of abject failure. Piling on the rewards can increase the pressure in the volcanoes of explosive children to the point that may lead to them exploding.

The other big downside of rewards is that, like punishments, they also presume that the child is in full control of their behaviour but for some reason they are choosing to act in ways that are considered antisocial, defiant and rude. Once again, this is not the case for most children, particularly those with ADHD. The trouble here is that if they really want a reward that is on offer, but are simply not capable of the requested behaviour, they are always going to be disappointed. What happens when they consistently fail? They find themselves right back in the cycle of shame (see page 69). Rewards are OK if they are achievable and if they make children feel good, but often they are neither.

But what about when you really need to get a child to do

something – can't rewards give them a quick boost of dopamine to help get them started? I am asked this lots. And perhaps from the previous paragraph you've presumed that I am totally anti-rewards. I'm not. For children who are dopamine seeking, like those with ADHD, the offer of a small reward to get them started on a task they really don't want to do can be invaluable. But (and it's a big but), using rewards like this needs to be kept to a minimum. Why? Because the more you use them, the less effective they will be. They quickly lose their excitement.

Imagine if it was your birthday every day. You would soon get bored of it, even if you love birthday cake and receiving gifts. Rewards are the same. Keep them for the moments when you really, really need them and try to resist using them if there is any other way you can help your child to get started on something (or, indeed, finish it). My final point here is that if you offer a reward, it has to be relatively easy for your child to receive it. For instance, if they are struggling to complete their homework because they weren't paying attention in class at the time it was set and so they're unsure as to what they have to do, the offer of a reward for them to complete it is unhelpful. If, however, you would like them to tidy their room a little (and I mean a little – a very specific task, because attempting to tidy their whole room at once is impossible for children with ADHD), then offering to play a game of their choice together once they've done it is fine, as the task is far more achievable for them. If the goal you set is too far out of your child's reach, you run the risk of making their behaviour far worse when they have to deal with the resulting disappointment and feelings of failure, which often ends in explosion.

What about using rewards during the peak of explosive behaviour as a way to calm them down? This is something I would never advise. What you are doing here is akin to bribery: 'If you calm down I will give you something nice.' This is the very opposite of co-regulation. It teaches your child that you are unable to contain their feelings, or cope with them. The more this happens, the less likely they are to trust you and turn to you when they are struggling. While it may sometimes feel impossible helping children in the midst of a huge, explosive meltdown and we may wish for the behaviour to disappear, bribing them out of these states only makes it harder for us in the future, because without our co-regulation and containment their pressure builds even more, with no regular degassing, and a dangerous explosion will inevitably follow.

When I discuss this with parents they will often say, 'Really? Never? Is there honestly never a situation where you would try to use rewards during an explosive episode?' My answer here is, 'It depends on the situation.' If you are in a place where it is dangerous to allow your child the time and space they need for their behaviour to diffuse, or if you are in an emotional state where you have no room left in your container to take on board any of their emotions and feel that you yourself are close to exploding, then absolutely I would turn to rewards, or anything else that could distract them. If it's a true emergency, then, in my opinion, anything goes that causes the least harm to everybody. I'm a big fan of the parenting ideology of 'do the least harm'. Here, the least harm is absolutely to reward, distract and try to avoid. The real issue is that if this becomes one of your main approaches, it won't be effective when you really need it to be and you completely avoid co-regulation (see page 83). In short, you're making things much worse for both your child and yourself in the long run if you rely on rewards with any regularity.

The right-hand tree branch – emergency discipline

What exactly should you do when your child is on the cusp of or in the midst of explosive behaviour? In the previous chapter we discussed two of the three parts of my behaviour tree; the roots and trunk (you) and the left-hand branch (understanding and preventing explosive behaviour). This chapter deals with the right-hand branch of 'emergency discipline', or what to do 'in the moment', when your child is mid-meltdown and their behaviour is out of control.

Although I can't promise you any magic solutions, I do have a well-tried-and-tested four-point plan that I want to share with you. I call these four points my ABCD of emergency discipline:

1. Alert to safety
2. Be calm
3. Co-regulation
4. De-escalation

Alert to safety

Safety has to come first. It doesn't matter how calm or gentle you are with your child if they are about to run into oncoming traffic or they break a glass vase on a baby's head. Safety trumps everything else and has to be your starting point.

What should you think about here?

- Start by taking a quick visual scan of the situation and environment. What action can you take that will ensure the most safety in the shortest period of time? For instance, if your child is about to hurt another child, will it be quicker to physically move them, or the other child? Or put yourself in between them?
- If your child is near something fragile, or something that they could hurt themselves on, then don't be afraid to physically move them away from it.
- If you are somewhere public, or in a room with lots of other people, perhaps at a family member's or friend's

house, then try to find somewhere private, quieter and calmer. Move your child to a space where they (and you) don't have to deal with onlookers or other children (including siblings) who may antagonise them and make their dysregulation worse.

- It's OK to leave the room if that is what will keep you calm and safe. It is better that you take some time to step away and breathe temporarily, so you are able to come back calmer, than to stay and end up yelling, or worse. Similarly, your child may want to be alone; if this is the case, then respect their need for privacy.

Once you have put safety measures into place (and only then), it is time to move on to the next step: calming yourself.

Be calm

Remember that you are a role model for your child, and a container for their dysregulated emotions. Ideally, you will have worked on your own container in advance (see Chapter Ten for more on this), so that you have space ready for your child's explosions. In reality, though, life happens, and there will be times when you are 'full up' and your child is also dysregulated (this is no coincidence – children are far more perceptive and tuned into our feelings than we realise). If you find the red mist rising and feel yourself being triggered by your child, it's time to take some deep breaths and remind yourself that you are the adult in this situation and your child needs you to be as calm as possible. That doesn't mean they need you to be perfect – it just means they need you to try your hardest. I find the best way to calm myself is to remember that, however much it may feel otherwise, my child is not behaving in this way on purpose and, in all likelihood, they feel far worse than I do.

Co-regulation

In the previous chapter we discussed co-regulation at length, all about how your presence can help your child to regulate their own emotions. I won't repeat what we discussed, but please do flick back to page 83 for a quick recap.

De-escalation

Once you are feeling calm and your child is beginning to co-regulate with you, the final step in my ABCD of emergency discipline is to work on de-escalating your child or helping them to fully calm down. Again, they may prefer privacy to do this. If this is the case, give them space, rather than trying to force them to sit with you (there will be plenty of time for that later). Try also to keep siblings away, until they feel ready to be around others again.

If your child is sensory seeking or avoiding, try to alter the immediate environment to suit them. For instance, can you reduce the noise (or carry some ear defenders with you), play their favourite music, adjust the lighting and remove or add smells? If you are out in public in an overwhelming sensory environment (such as a brightly lit, noisy shopping centre or mall), try to find somewhere quiet and dimly lit or get outside if you can.

If your child is younger, get down to their level to talk, rather than towering over them. Use a calm, quiet, non-threatening voice and let them know that you want to help. Note – this doesn't mean you are excusing their behaviour or ignoring anything they have done; it just means you are showing that you want to work with them, collaboratively, not against them. When you do speak, use short, simple sentences. Don't talk too much – they will not be in a position to hear what you have to say if you end up going into lecture mode. Try to stay patient and give them as much time as possible to regulate. Time pressures will only make things worse, and if you try to make them hurry up, inevitably it will end up taking even longer until they reach a state of being regulated enough that you can continue with your plans.

Remind your child of some techniques they use to help regulate, such as a specific breathing technique (more on this soon) or playing with a fiddle toy. Finally, reassure them that you are on their side and that you want to help. Giving them this validation will help with their self-esteem and, ultimately, improve the impact of co-regulation with you in the future.

When your child is fully calm (and you are, too), talk through what you both could have done differently to help, and make a plan for next time.

Some quick calming techniques

I am a huge advocate of teaching your child some simple calming techniques. However, there are three very important caveats here:

1. The most effective calming techniques will be ones that are familiar. This means practising them lots when calm. The worst thing you can suggest to anybody who is in a state of hyperarousal or hypervigilance is to try a new soothing technique because the very opposite will happen. It will be too much for them to focus on and it will add to their dysregulation. Calming techniques are something to discuss with your child when they (and you) are calm. And the more they practise them, the better – they need to feel like old and trusty reliable friends when the time comes to use them.

2. Don't attempt to promote the use of any calming techniques when your child is consumed by anger, frustration, fear or anything else that has triggered an explosive episode. When they are in a state of fight or flight and their body is flooded with adrenaline and cortisol, they are physically unable to focus on any calming technique, or even your voice. Again, you need to wait. Keep them safe, keep yourself safe, focus on co-regulation and when the explosion starts to dissipate, then you can encourage them to use one of their well-tested calming techniques.

3. Some children with ADHD will struggle to focus on mental calming or mindfulness techniques and this struggle may make them feel even more dysregulated and frustrated. If this is the case for your child, please don't try to push things. Trying to relax in this instance is going to have completely the opposite effect. Find something that works for them, usually of a more physical than mental nature (such as those towards the end of the suggestions below).

Here are some techniques that may help your child (and you) to calm down after an explosion. It's very much about personal preference, so don't be afraid to try something completely different if it works for your family.

The petrol gauge

Imagine a car petrol gauge (showing your child some photographs or drawing a quick cartoon of one can help if they struggle to picture one). Note where the needle is when the car is full of petrol and where it is when it is empty. Imagine that the full end is coloured red and the empty end is coloured green, with orange in the middle.

The full/red end indicates being full of rage, stress and frustration and the empty/green end indicates calmness. Encourage your child to try to imagine slowly moving the needle from the full/red end to the empty/green end and, as they do so, to imagine all the stressful emotions leaving their body.

The volcano and the fire extinguisher

Ask your child to draw a volcano (or draw one for them if they are not keen on art) and to imagine the magma rising inside it and lava erupting over the edges in fiery red.

Next, encourage them to imagine a fire extinguisher. If you have one in your home (which you probably should have!), you can show it to them; if not, look for some videos of fire extinguishers in use online. When they have an explosion, and their behaviour starts to calm a little, enough so that they can hear what you're saying, encourage them to imagine a giant fire extinguisher putting out all the flames and cooling the lava into a cold, smooth black rock. This works extra well if you can source a piece of basalt or obsidian for them to hold and feel in their fingers at the same time.

Box breathing

This technique is intended to help your child focus on their breathing, and works in two ways: it helps to take attention away from difficult emotions, and also to trick the brain into thinking that they are calm and safe.

Box breathing simply involves breathing in deeply through the nose for a count of four, holding to a count of four, then breathing out through the nose for a count of four, before waiting for another count of four to begin the cycle again. Alongside this, your child can imagine a square in their mind or trace a square in the air with their finger. Start in the bottom left-hand corner and move up as they breathe in, as they hold for four, move to the right, as they breathe out, move down and then, as they hold, move left back to the starting position.

I-spy senses

If your child enjoys playing 'I spy', they may enjoy this one. This is a form of meditation to focus them on their surroundings and help them to feel more grounded. Encourage them to think of:

- five things they can see
- four things they can touch
- three things they can hear
- two things they can smell
- one thing they can taste.

This activity is usually best done with you prompting them.

Countdown

This one is very simple for older children with good counting abilities. Encourage them to start at a high number, such as one or two hundred and count down to zero. The idea here is that it is hard to focus on anything else aside from the backwards counting. Do be aware, though, that this is really a Marmite one, and can be very hard for some children, especially if they have dyscalculia or struggle with maths.

Birthday-cake candles

This one can be magic for younger children. When everybody is calm, set up some small tealight or birthday candles and encourage your child to blow them all out, one at a time. Explain to them that if they can remember how it felt to blow out the candles and can picture them in their mind, it can help if they are feeling triggered. Instead of simply imagining blowing out the candles, encourage them to inflate their cheeks and blow steadily, until they feel that all the candles are blown out, or they no longer feel the need for the exercise.

Jumping jacks

For children who really need to move to release big feelings, encourage them to perform as many jumping jacks (sometimes called star jumps) as they need to feel some of the tension leaving their body. If they are not feeling overstimulated from a sensory perspective, playing their favourite music in the background can help, too.

Fingertip taps

Fingertip taps involve tapping each of the fingers with the thumb, one at a time. Start by tapping the thumb and index finger together, then move on to the middle finger and thumb, then the ring finger and thumb and finally the little finger and thumb. They can either do both hands simultaneously or one at a time. Repeat for as long as it is helping.

No calming technique is magic, but if you can find one or two that work for your child, they can be incredibly helpful for calming after an explosion. And eventually, they may also play a positive role in degassing and prevention, too.

Taking some time to chat with your child when you are both calm and brainstorming some calming techniques together is also a great way to show them that you are really on their side. Encourage them to try out any techniques that they feel may help them and report back to you on their effectiveness afterwards. Some of these may help them for many years, while some may help only temporarily, so do take some time to discuss and assess together every now and again. If your child is at school, be sure also to chat with their teacher (or form tutor, if they are in secondary or high school). This way, teachers can make a note of techniques that may help your child, so that they can suggest them if necessary; but also, importantly, it means that your child is supported in utilising them. We'll discuss school in more detail in Chapter Six.

The power of nature

One thing we haven't considered so far in the book that can be incredibly helpful for children with ADHD and explosive behaviour is spending more time outside, in nature. One of my favourite quotes, by author Erin K. Kenny, is: 'If children are bouncing off the walls, then take the walls away.' And it is true many children will struggle to stay calm when they are cooped up inside all day. For my family, getting outside instantly calmed us all. Flynn used to love to climb trees and would sit for ages perching on a branch. If we were really struggling, one of my first coping techniques was to put us all into warm and waterproof clothing (or sunhats and sunscreen, depending on the season) and to get outside. We would visit a local park as often as possible and spent many hours on long walks and in local forests. We are lucky in that we live rurally; however, you can get closer to nature wherever you are. The prerequisites really are just a big, open outdoor space, some grass, hopefully a tree or two, and the ability to run, move and jump and, preferably, climb.

Research looking at the behaviour of children with ADHD has found that those who spend more time outside in green spaces show significantly less explosive behaviour than their peers who spend more time indoors.[1] Interestingly, studies have even found that just having a view of green open space increases impulse control and better behaviour in children, compared to those who live in a city, with no view of nature.[2] While you can't change the view outside your window, if you do live in a city, you could consider the impact of nature in your décor, perhaps by displaying nature pictures on your walls.

Shinrin-yoku

Loosely translated as 'forest bathing' or simply spending time outside surrounded by trees, I have always found the Japanese concept of shinrin-yoku fascinating. Research indicates that this has enormous benefits for everybody when it comes to reducing stress levels, which is not only helpful for your child, but for you, too.[3] Time spent in this way helps to reduce blood pressure, improves mental health, reduces depression and improves immunity, as well as attention.[4] The beauty of spending time in forests, or wooded areas in a local park if you do not live near one, is that the experience can be entirely tailored to the needs of the child at that particular time. Whether they need to move or be still, be loud or be quiet, have more sensory input or less, the forest provides opportunities for all of these. And perhaps best of all, time in nature is usually free.

If I could turn back the clock and change something about how I raised my own children, I would definitely spend even more time in nature than we already did.

Supporting siblings

As we near the end of this chapter, I wanted to divert a little and spend some time discussing ways to support siblings of children with ADHD and explosive behaviour. Seeing your other child, or children, struggling because of their brother's or sister's behaviour is so distressing and can also be a huge source of stress, filling your container to the brim.

I have four children, three of whom are neurotypical. Learning to balance Flynn's needs with those of his siblings has been a steep learning curve. In the early years I frequently found myself refereeing arguments and feeling guilty for spending so little time with them, instead focusing on Flynn's needs, especially during his school years. I felt sad that his siblings missed out on events that Flynn would find difficult, and mortified when their friends complained to them about their brother. That said, the heartbreak at watching Flynn struggle with things that his siblings found easy, or seeing him at their birthday parties with lots of friends, after a year in which not one single child had turned up to his, sometimes felt like too much to bear.

I think the best piece of advice I could give you here is to never compare your children. They all have their own gifts and talents; they all do things at different rates; and they all have their own unique life path. They don't have to be the same, or even similar. Recognising and accepting them for who they are is so important. I would also recommend teaching your other child, or children, about ADHD as soon as possible. As they grow, they can become your neurodivergent child's biggest advocates, supporters and champions.

As we learned in Chapter One, there is a strong hereditary component to ADHD, and it is possible that more than one of your children has it. Often, it isn't until a sibling is diagnosed that parents realise that their other child, or children, are also neurodivergent. Sometimes siblings are both, or all (if you have more than two children) diagnosed with ADHD; other times they are diagnosed with a co-existing condition, such as autism. Just as we discussed in Chapter One, if you do feel instinctively that you have another child who may be neurodivergent, I would strongly recommend trusting your gut and looking into pursuing a diagnosis for them.

You are probably surrounded with images and videos of happy families on social media, where siblings delight in each other's company. However, siblings often fight and fall out, and I think part of the issue here is when reality does not reflect our expectations and our feelings. Simply put, don't expect your children to be the best of friends when they are younger. Tricky sibling relationships are normal, even among neurotypical children. In fact, these sibling squabbles can teach important skills about relationships and conflict management. While it may feel terrible to see them fighting or to come to the realisation that they may not like each other very much, in my experience, the relationships and bonds grow and strengthen as they get older and understand each other more.

My final sibling tip is to try to spend time individually with each of your children as often as possible. You don't have to make grand gestures or have expensive days out – just grasp any opportunity that you can. Even a one-hour trip to the supermarket provides much-needed one-to-one reconnection and attention. I found this especially important for my other children when my attention had been firmly focused on Flynn for some time. While they were understanding during the hospital appointments and constant meetings at school, they did struggle with losing some of the time and connection with me. I tried hard, therefore, to always set something up with them once things had calmed down a little, to try to make up for the lost time, and also to show them that they were equally as important to me, even if they didn't always have equal amounts of my time.

Raising multiple neurotypical children is hard work. Raising one or more neurodivergent children and trying to balance their needs with those of their siblings can often feel impossible. I wish I could wave a magic wand and give you a solution here – but I just can't. I found balancing sibling needs (and my guilt when I couldn't) possibly the hardest role when my children were younger. All I can say here is to give yourself grace. It feels hard because it is hard – not because you are somehow failing as a parent. We'll delve into this much more in Chapters Nine and Ten. But what I will say for now is that things do get easier as your children get older and the sibling relationships that feel fraught and difficult now really can blossom into something quite beautiful in the future.

Rupture and repair

An explosive episode can leave everybody feeling exhausted and emotionally wrung out. In Chapter Ten we'll talk lots about the guilt and regret that parents can feel over the way they have handled things, and how to deal with any residual anger or resentment towards your child. What I'd like to focus on now, however, is the idea of reconnecting with your child and making things right after the explosive behaviour has ruptured your relationship. Psychologists call this process 'rupture and repair'.

Can you remember a time from your own childhood when you behaved in a way that made your parents angry? Perhaps they shouted at you, banished you to your room, cancelled a special treat that was planned, or maybe they responded with physical violence. Regarding the latter, incidentally if you are a child of the 1970s, 80s or 90s, then it is highly likely that you were on the receiving end of a smack if you angered your parents. Research has found that even in 2011, over 40 per cent of parents in the UK admitted to smacking their children as a form of discipline.[5] Anyway, think back to a time when you had been deemed to be 'naughty' and were punished or chastised for it. What happened afterwards – after the punishment was carried out? Did your parents talk to you and apologise for overreacting? Did they tell you that actually, it wasn't your fault? Did they show you empathy and real understanding? Did they give you a hug and try to make things right?

When I give talks to parents, I ask the audience to raise their hands if they remember being apologised to by their parents or carers as a child. Barely any hands go up. In fact, I'm often greeted with perplexed looks. Why would an adult apologise to a child if the child has misbehaved? Most of us were raised to believe that adults are always right and children are always wrong, and that children should always treat adults with respect. The problem here is that the respect is rarely a two-way thing. Adults do get things wrong, and children deserve respect, too. If, as adults, we get things wrong – if we overreact or fail to consider our child's point of view – then why on earth would we not apologise to them?

Rupture and repair is all about apologising and making things right. It's about showing children that we do respect them (and showing them respect is, in fact, the best way to encourage them to respect us) and that we care about how they feel. It is also about being honest and owning our mistakes. We know that children with ADHD are prone to rejection sensitive dysphoria and entering the cycle of shame (see pages 32 and 69). But if we own up to our mistakes and take time to repair the relationship, we avoid both of these and make co-regulation far more likely to be successful. It is in everybody's best interest to repair the rupture. We'll talk about this more in Chapter Ten, because it's also important that you don't place pressure on yourself to always get it right, especially if you are neurodivergent yourself. It's OK to screw up, so long as you try to make it right afterwards.

*

In an ideal world, focusing on the trunk and roots (you) and the left-hand branch (understanding and preventing triggers) of the behaviour tree will reduce the likelihood of explosions. That said, explosions are still inevitable. So the next time you feel an out-of-control situation arising, try to remember the ABCDs of 'emergency discipline':

- Alert to safety
- Be calm
- Co-regulation
- De-escalation

Knowing how to de-escalate and help your child through explosive episodes with a focus on emergency discipline and safety, and then restoring your relationship (through rupture and repair) is arguably the kindest and most effective way to approach raising children with ADHD and undiagnosed explosive behaviour. Let's move on now to the next chapter, which is all about navigating education and what to do when difficulties arise.

Chapter Six

ADHD, explosive behaviour and education

'Sarah, do you think ADHD and mainstream state schooling can ever mix?'

I cannot tell you how many times I've been asked this question. And my answer to it has varied hugely, depending on what I was going through in my own personal life. If you had asked me when Flynn first started school, at the age of five, when his days were filled with play, crafts and nature with a nurturing and understanding teacher, I would have said, 'Yes, of course!' with no hesitation. Fast-forward to secondary school, during a particularly rough time, when it felt like the whole school was against Flynn and I was called into meetings or by telephone on an almost daily basis, I would have answered with a resounding 'No!' Now, retrospectively, I think my answer is a more nuanced 'It depends . . .'

What I will say is that school is almost certainly far more of a struggle for children with ADHD and undiagnosed explosive behaviour – and their parents – than it is for neurotypical children. As a parent, you have to be ready to fight for your child and their rights. You have to have the container space to mop up a lot of overflowing and overwhelming feelings and still have space left for constant conversations with school staff. The education system (in the UK, at least) is just not designed with the needs of neurodivergent children in mind. I would even go so far as to say that it is not designed with the needs of any children in mind – however, neurotypical children are far better equipped to navigate it. Many of the thirteen years Flynn spent in state schooling felt like a constant uphill struggle, trying to fit a square peg into a round hole, with professionals constantly blaming me as the cause of the poor fit. Would I have done things differently if I'd known then what I know now? I'm not sure. Flynn himself wouldn't change anything and that is perhaps more important than my own feelings.

I'm quite aware that I have started this chapter off on a negative note, and I apologise for that. I suspect, however, that you have already had negative experiences, and likely share my opinions and frustrations. I also need to let you know that the negativity is going to continue for several more pages before I switch to empowering you and your child and focusing on how they can thrive through these years. My aim for this chapter is not to convince you that school is wrong for your child, because I strongly believe that all children (and, indeed, schools) are different and there is no right or wrong answer when it comes to education for children with ADHD and those with explosive but undiagnosed behaviour. What I would like to do, however, is to talk through common sticking points – such as school discipline and behaviour-management techniques, masking, dealing with difficult behaviour at home that has been held in all day and homework woes – and, hopefully, equip you to deal with these as easily as possible.

If your child isn't yet at school, or you are soon making the move up to secondary or high school, you will find some help here for choosing a school that will most suit your child. We will also talk about alternatives to school for those who obviously need, or want, something different, with the aim that you and your child together can feel comfortable in knowing that the choices made around their education are the best for them and your family.

What I am not going to do in this chapter is delve into the legalities of education provision and the ins and outs of seeking specialist support or an Education, Health and Care Plan (EHCP) for your child. These things differ, depending on where you are in the world and, hopefully, change is afoot, meaning that this book will likely not be the most up-to-date source of information for you in this respect. Again, however, I have listed some good sources of support at the back of the book for you (see Resources, page 223).

The trouble with most school behaviour management

When I talk about discipline, I often refer to the Latin root word *discere*, which means 'to learn'. *Discere* further gives us the Latin noun *disciplina*, which is used to imply teaching and education. Discipline, in the true sense of the word, should be about teaching children to have respectful relationships with others and how to behave in more socially acceptable ways. As part of this teaching, adults should seek to understand children, and any hurdles standing in their way, so that their education can be tailored to their needs. Only when this understanding and, indeed, mutual respect is in place does true learning happen. The very fact that so many working in education refer to discipline as 'behaviour management' tells you all you need to know. That it isn't truly about helping children, but managing them, like a form of crowd control.

Just like the traditional mainstream discipline techniques we spoke about in the past two chapters the cornerstones of school behaviour management are punishment and reward. If a child is well behaved, they are rewarded with praise, certificates, 'star-of-the-week' awards, happy clouds, green traffic lights or behaviour ladders displayed on the classroom walls, dojo points, headteacher commendations, celebration ceremonies and the like. If they are poorly behaved, they are punished, although most schools prefer to call these punishments 'consequences' (I would imagine because it makes the illogical punishments sound more logical and modern). These consequences range from moving the child on to a sad cloud or the bottom rung of the behaviour ladder, like a miserable game of snakes and ladders, to removing them from the class temporarily (for example, sending them to see the headteacher), lunchtime or after-school detentions, isolation (where they are sent to a room or a booth for a form of solitary confinement) and, in extreme cases, exclusion or expulsion.

The problems with every single one of these techniques are threefold:

1. **They all presume the child is in full control of their behaviour.** The idea here is that the child is consciously choosing to behave poorly and therefore, either through the promise of a reward or the threat of punishment, they will be motivated to behave better. Behaviour is reduced to the overly simplistic notion of children making 'poor choices'.

2. **They all presume the child has everything they need to improve their behaviour.** Following on from the previous point, this assumes that motivation is the only sticking point, and that children have everything they need, physically, emotionally and cognitively to improve their behaviour at will. It also assumes that there are no underlying issues that need to be solved and that nothing at school needs to change – only the child.

3. **They are highly discriminatory for children with ADHD and co-existing conditions.** Many of the behaviours that children with ADHD are punished for are symptoms of ADHD – for instance, not sitting still, not paying attention in class, forgetting equipment, forgetting to do homework, calling out in class and similar. Can you think of any other condition where children are actively punished for the manifestations? For instance, would we punish a child with vision problems for not copying down something written on a blackboard? Would we punish a child with mobility problems for struggling to take part in a PE lesson? Would we punish a child with hearing problems for not being able to repeat something just spoken about in class? If we would consider punishing a child for any of these discriminatory, then why is it OK for schools to punish children with ADHD for symptoms that are directly related to their ADHD?

Regarding the final point, I have always found it nonsensical that schools so frequently dish out consequences of lunchtime detentions to children with hyperactivity and explosive behaviour. These children need to run and move and let off steam at lunchtime, just as much as they need food. By keeping them cooped up in a classroom instead, the school is almost guaranteeing further problematic behaviour and an escalation to even more severe consequences.

The obsession with giving consequences as the mainstay of school behaviour management is, sadly, not the only form of discrimination children with ADHD face at school. Stigma still abounds among many staff. You only have to visit X (formerly Twitter) and read discussions among some teachers, which usually end quickly in conclusions that 1. they believe ADHD is grossly overdiagnosed and often just an excuse for poor behaviour, 2. that there is too much focus on 'new-age, airy-fairy' restorative approaches to discipline, trauma and unmet needs and 3. that poor behaviour is a parenting problem. These same teachers will often advocate for increasing medication dosages, so that children are more easily controlled and quiet at school, and they frequently call for more expulsions for their most difficult students.

I know I sound anti-teacher here. I am not. I am a huge champion of teachers. They are underpaid, underappreciated and overworked. I don't believe that they are uncaring or that they mean to be discriminatory. They have just reached the end of their tethers in a system that is not designed to meet the needs of the children in it. There is not enough time or money for the big changes that really need to happen, and teachers are left firefighting without the necessary resources or support. It is understandable that they end up blaming parents, while parents blame them, when, in fact, the real problems are our governments, politicians and educational policymakers. My eldest child is a state secondary schoolteacher and I know how tough it is. I see that his empathy and passion make a difference to the children he teaches, and I also see the exhaustion and regret when he realises he can't always be the educator he really wants to be. I am not naïve, but something has to change. The fact that some teachers are publicly calling for children with ADHD to be pushed out of the school system to make things easier for them and the other students in the class is unbelievably problematic. Where does the segregation end? Which group of children will be discriminated against next?

Aside from discrimination, the other big issue with school behaviour management is that it clearly doesn't work. Over the last decade in the UK, there has been a strong move towards 'zero-tolerance' behaviour policies, largely spearheaded by the government appointing a 'behaviour tsar', who is a huge fan of behaviourism and not impressed at all by the idea that there is always a reason behind difficult behaviour. The irony here is that nothing has improved. In fact, things appear to be getting worse. In a recent survey, a whopping 97 per cent of teachers said they struggled with difficult verbal behaviour from students and over a third had faced physical violence or damage to property from students at some point.[1] The zero-tolerance approaches are obviously not working, yet the leading proponents continue to double down on their views and blame either the parents or those who advocate a more holistic approach to school discipline for 'watering down' their recommended approach. If the current consequences-based behaviour-management techniques worked, we would not see the same children in detentions and isolations repeatedly or a disproportionate number of children with ADHD and other special educational needs excluded from school. Any behaviour-management approach that focuses solely on firefighting, or what I refer to as emergency discipline, is doomed to fail if there is not also a focus on the relationships, co-regulation and teacher wellbeing. Alongside all this, there needs to be a serious look into the issues faced by children at school and a change to the way things work to better suit their needs, rather than forcing all of them to fit into the fractured and failing system.

Something has to change, not just for the children, but for teachers too. Alarmingly, in the UK, 10 per cent of teachers said they have been physically assaulted by students within the last year. This is clearly not OK. As I mentioned at the start of this section, I think most teachers are superheroes and they have a right to go to work and expect to be safe. They do not deserve to be hit, shouted at, sworn at or have things thrown at them. Similarly, though, we cannot continue discriminating against children with ADHD and other undiagnosed explosive behaviour just because there are no other easy options or quick fixes. We need to stop trying to force square-peg children into round holes and instead make holes into which any shape will fit, providing a truly inclusive education for all.

EQUITY VS EQUALITY

Many people believe that all children should be treated fairly at school. What they really mean when they say that is that all children should be treated the same, with the same opportunities, and indeed the same behaviour policies applied to them. The trouble is that actually, it is grossly unfair. True fairness is not giving every child the same thing but giving them what they need – and needs vary hugely from child to child.

What I am advocating for here is a school-discipline system based upon equity, not the equality it is currently based upon. Equality means treating each and every child in the same way, with equal rights and equal opportunities. This would be good if all children were able to grasp these opportunities and did not have anything holding them back. But if you treat a child with ADHD in the same way as a neurotypical child, you are immediately putting them at a disadvantage because you are not considering that their executive-function skills are not developed to the same degree as their neurotypical peers'. What happens then is that you are setting them up to fail. Instead, if we go with an equity-based approach, we consider these differences and needs and make reasonable adjustments to allow children with ADHD to start off on an equal footing to their peers. It is only when we use an equity-based approach to education, notably in behaviour management, that we do not discriminate against these children. Equity is not giving those with ADHD 'special treatment' or 'rewarding them for bad behaviour', as many mistakenly believe. It is taking away some of the barriers that they face on a daily basis to allow them to access education in the same way as their neurotypical peers. Only equity is truly fair.

Improving behaviour at school with alternative approaches

I find when I speak up about the problems with our education system, raising my concerns, especially those related to the treatment of children with ADHD, I'm immediately asked, 'Well, what would you do to change things, then?' Often, my answer isn't one that I think most want to hear because, once again, the issues run so deep that genuinely only a complete education and SEND reform could truly change things. Unfortunately, this looks unlikely, because this sort of change requires long-term thinking and investment from politicians, and a critical look at why things aren't working now. This all takes time and a tremendous amount of money – two things we don't have when we have hundreds of thousands of children currently going through the system and are in the midst of a cost-of-living crisis.

What, then, can you do? Here, I think we have to understand that any approach is going to be superficial, like a sticking plaster. Any attempt to change behaviour in a short period of time without significant investment into child-and-adolescent mental-health services, child-development and healthcare services, the social-security or benefits system and a serious attempt to improve the workload of teachers and stop the teacher recruitment-and-retention crisis is never going to give the results that parents, carers and school staff (and, indeed, politicians) alike want to see. We have to start with recognising this and aiming for small, achievable goals.

If I took over as the governmental behaviour tsar tomorrow, this is what I would at least work towards implementing:

- We need to start with community, building bridges between teachers and parents, moving from a position of blaming each other, to recognising the bigger picture and researching ways in which we can work collaboratively and support each other with the enormous challenges we are facing.

- The focus needs to be on relationships, connection and allowing all children to feel a sense of belonging at school. I would start by creating a student advisory council in every school, giving students the opportunity to comment on school policies, feed back their experiences and suggest different ways of working. This council should be formed of both neuro-typical and neurodivergent children, as well as those from other minority backgrounds, allowing genuine representation.

- I would set up a mandatory training programme for all school staff and all those who work in education policy and education-related government organisations to ensure that all adults have a thorough understanding of ADHD (and other co-existing conditions), especially focusing on the neurobiological component. The provision for this in teacher training is currently woefully lacking and far too many teachers, governors, trust managers and government workers rely on their own (often ill-informed) opinions of ADHD, rather than scientific fact and education based on lived experience. It is vital that the stigma is removed and the resulting discrimination is stopped.

- I would introduce a child-and-adolescent psychology component to all PGCE (post-graduate certificate in education) teacher-training courses. This module should last for at least half a term, preferably a whole one, and involve in-depth training on attachment theory, adverse childhood experiences and trauma, co-regulation and the impact of the carer on the development of these. Far too much lip service is paid to child development in the education sector and understanding is often superficial at best.

- I would run regular personal, social, health and economic (PSHE) sessions on neurodivergence, including specific conditions, so that all pupils develop a good understanding of the hurdles some of their peers are facing and how they can help them. Ideally, these would be run by staff with special training and experience (for example, the special educational needs co-ordinator – SENCo), those with lived experience (for example staff who have ADHD or are autistic), neurodivergent alumni, or specialist external speakers (if funds stretch). This would also help all pupils to understand the difference between equality and equity and would mean the end of viewing some children as 'getting special treatment'.

- I would have a buddy system for all children with ADHD (and other co-existing conditions), preferably with older ones who have experienced the same conditions and would like to share things that helped them with younger children. These buddies would act as unofficial mentors, listening ears, and also take children under their wings at playtime if they are struggling with forming friendships. This system would not only benefit the mentee, but the mentor, too.

- I would ensure all children have access to time in nature at school, providing more for those who need it most (for example, those struggling with ADHD and explosive behaviour), instead of more time being shut in a classroom. I would set up more wildlife areas, school allotments and wooded areas for children and, if this were not possible, I would seek to use local amenities. I would add bushcraft and forest-school sessions throughout the entirety of their education, from infant school to sixth form.

- I would create a wellbeing hub in each school, providing a room (preferably two or three) staffed by a wellbeing co-ordinator with special training in SEND and neurodivergence and child and adolescent mental health. This person would have an open-door policy for children who needed to speak to them at any time. Those children with ADHD and explosive behaviour would be given a 'wellbeing pass', allowing them to leave the classroom and visit the hub at any time. The hub would also contain a quiet sensory room for those children struggling to regulate their emotions. This should be viewed not as 'time out', but a sanctuary for a child in need. There should be no chastisement or telling off by school staff, and no discipline when they return to the class from the sensory room, just a recognition of need.

- I would introduce more movement into the school day, starting or ending it (or both) with fun exercise (preferably outdoors) and providing opportunities to move during lessons for children who need to. Children would never have lunchtime detentions, this time being protected for rest, recuperation, play and movement.

- For those in secondary or high school, I would allow them to pursue alternative lessons in creative, sport-based or employment-focused subjects. Children do not all need to aim for a flurry of exams in traditional academic subjects and forcing them to do so is not in anybody's best interests. Instead, I would focus on the core subjects, such as mathematics and English, while encouraging a broader, more holistic curriculum for those who are most likely to benefit from it. Every child should have the opportunity to flourish and thrive in something that they enjoy and are good at.

- I would provide a nutritious, freshly cooked breakfast and lunch for every child at school, free of charge. Obviously, this would require a significant amount of money, but the impact of this on children of all ages, including adolescents, would likely reduce spending further down the line.
- I would stop all consequences (and by this, what I mean is punishments masquerading as consequences). There would be a zero-tolerance approach to violence (towards other students and school staff) and there would be a culture of mutual respect throughout the whole school instead. School rules would be significantly thinned out and new ones written in collaboration with students. Antisocial and disruptive behaviour would be dealt with restoratively, through a lens of curiosity, with non-judgemental conversations with specially trained teachers, whereby staff seek to uncover the causes of dysregulation and work with children to overcome problems preventing them from displaying the respectful behaviour that the school expects.
- I would move away from the overuse of rewards and shallow praise, and towards a system of showing appreciation, gratitude and encouragement. These would not only be given by teaching staff, but anybody in the school (including admin and support staff, the management and leadership team, maintenance staff and fellow students) through a nomination and recognition system.
- Students would take on more roles and responsibilities in the day-to-day running of the school, giving them a sense of pride and ownership. Those children with

ADHD and explosive behaviour should especially be tasked with responsibilities that involve movement and make use of their creative skills.

- Books and equipment would be kept in classrooms as standard for any children who struggle with organisation skills and short-term memory, so taking the pressure off for them to remember and organise themselves for every lesson.

- There would be more opportunities for co-regulation with school staff for those students who are struggling, particularly with specially trained members of the pastoral team.

- There would be a focus on structure and routine, with as few differentiations to this as possible. If change was unavoidable, those children with ADHD and other conditions which lead to explosive behaviour would be supported and helped with this in advance, where possible.

- Each classroom would have a selection of sensory tools for children to use if they needed to and every teacher would have a good knowledge of how these could be utilised. And during PSHE sessions, all pupils would be taught about equity and would understand why only some of their fellow students would be able to use them, rather than having free access to them for all.

- One session lasting no more than thirty minutes per week would be given over to teaching all students about social skills, relationships, altruism and acceptance and creating social allies. This would primarily be done through a scheme of sharing fiction books, watching cartoons and videos, art activities and discussion points with class teachers and form tutors.

- I would encourage more playfulness throughout the whole curriculum, at all ages.

- Finally, I would introduce meditation and mindfulness sessions as standard at least once a week, not only for students, but for all school staff, too.

I am aware, of course, that this is an incredibly ambitious list. However, many of the elements are straightforward to implement with little time or financial investment required.

The question I would always ask is: if schools are spending so much time (and money) trying to tackle behaviour through outdated and ineffective methods that make everybody (adults included) feel bad, then doesn't it seem ridiculous not to at least try something different? Change requires bravery, but unless we have more brave people, behaviour is going to continue to worsen as staff morale continues to dip. For me, making no change is the riskier choice.

Masking at school

One element of explosive behaviour that we haven't considered so far in this chapter is when it only happens at home. This can be so hard for parents who struggle with out-of-control behaviour at home and yet when they raise it with the school, they can't see a problem. In these instances, it is insinuated that the issue is really a parenting one. And if the children are well behaved at school and poorly behaved at home, I can understand why many will believe this to be the case. However, it is far more likely that the issue is that the child is masking at school. This is markedly common in girls with ADHD.

Children can become adept at learning how to behave at school by watching their peers, and they work hard to contain all their feelings, maintaining the illusion that they are coping well. At parents' evenings, teachers will often say that they are no bother at all in class, although they could participate a little more, by asking and answering more questions. Sometimes they will say that your child seems to daydream a lot, but they are an easy, well-behaved student and they have no concerns. If you raise the issue of their explosive behaviour at home, this is often met with disbelief. This can be especially problematic if you are seeking a diagnosis, as the behaviour needs to be observable in at least two different settings. The school will be asked to complete some observation questionnaires as part of the process, too. So, if you suspect that your child is masking at school, my best advice here would be to discuss this with their teachers and encourage them to welcome some more authentic behaviour from your child by letting them know that they are in a safe place.

Explosions that happen at home after a day at school are often referred to as 'after-school restraint collapse'. This term is not entirely accurate, though, as they can happen at any time – in the morning before school, at weekends and during school holidays. Regardless of when they take place, however, the best way to handle them is to acknowledge what is happening: that your child feels safe with you to let their feelings out. When you realise that you are being a container for their emotions and helping them to co-regulate, then you will not view the behaviour negatively or take it personally.

One day, I hope we will live in a world where no children have after-school restraint collapse and, instead, we have an education system that meets the needs of all children. Until then, we can help by understanding what is happening for our children and provide them with a sanctuary at home.

Homework woes

If your child is young, you probably haven't had to navigate trying to encourage them to do their homework; if they are older, then I'm sure you're well versed in the difficulties. I have found the best way to cope with homework issues is to get to the root cause of them and provide your child with as much support and scaffolding as possible. Here are a few ideas that can help.

Routine and structure

This could be arranging a regular homework time (for instance, between 5 and 6 p.m. every night), encouraging always doing it in the same place (for instance, at your dining table), having a homework routine (for instance, starting with a snack, dancing to music for a minute or two to energise the brain and calm the body and then sitting with a special cushion).

Make sure they understand what they should be doing

Very often, homework refusal and procrastination happen because the child doesn't know how to start. Maybe they didn't note down what they needed to do, how they should do it or know when it should be given in. If your child struggles with things like this, you could ask their teachers to note down the homework for them in a planner each time it is set.

Organise their study space

Making a specific study space and stocking it with common supplies that your child needs can be really helpful, especially if they struggle to start because they don't have a pen, a pencil, a ruler, a glue stick or other necessary items of stationery. Rather than them packing these things away in their room, or their bag, keep them in a 'study-supplies box', which stays in the same place, ready to use.

Reduce distractions

This may sound obvious, but it's so rare that we do it. If your child has a mobile phone, this isn't the time for them to have it with them. Ditto their laptop or a tablet, unless their work has to be done online. Encourage them to think about the best environment for them to study in – for instance, do they do best in silence (in which case some noise-cancelling ear buds can help) or do they study better with background music?

Body doubling

Body doubling refers to the interesting phenomenon of people with ADHD finding it easier to get started on a task and, importantly, complete it, if they have somebody else with them. This doesn't mean that the other person is helping, or even conversing with them, they could simply be in the same room but getting on with their own work, cooking dinner, cleaning windows or, in fact, doing anything. It is simply their presence that helps the individual to feel motivated and able to focus on their studies.

When your child refuses to attend school

Understandably, the difficulties and adversity faced at school can result in many children refusing to attend. A much better term for school refusal, however, is 'emotionally based school avoidance' (or EBSA).

The term EBSA helps parents, carers and school staff to understand that children who do not, or rather cannot, attend school are not just being difficult, obstinate, manipulative, defiant or simply naughty, but that their avoidance is underpinned by complex and often multiple wellbeing and mental-health reasons. While some children with EBSA are unable to attend school at all, some will be able to do so part-time, or sporadically. Much like our discussion on school discipline earlier in this chapter, punishing a child for EBSA or using rewards to attempt to bribe them into attendance isn't just ineffective, but can also do more damage to their emotional health by completely ignoring the underlying reasons for the EBSA. The common approach of systematic desensitisation or graduated-exposure therapy, where children are encouraged to attend school for increasingly short amounts of time, can be more helpful, but again, only if the underlying issues are worked with first and the child is fully supported (which, sadly, is often not the case).

There is no one cause of EBSA. Instead, the reasons are individual to each child. For children with ADHD and explosive behaviour, it is likely related to self-esteem issues and the constant pressure placed upon them to change, combined with the lack of understanding and support shown to them. Often, there are friendship or bullying issues, struggling to fit into their peer group or the sheer exhaustion of constantly masking daily. Sometimes there are co-existing conditions compounding the problems and often, there are also mental-health issues, including depression and anxiety. These are children who are already struggling, for whom attending school makes everything overwhelming, causing more trauma when they do go, or even just engage with things that are school related, such as wearing the uniform. EBSA is often accompanied by physical manifestations of anxiety and stress and fight or flight, including headaches, nausea, stomach upsets or lowered immunity, due to constant exposure to adrenaline and

cortisol. These only serve to compound the emotional symptoms and worries.

As we have seen several times already, working with children
with ADHD requires a collaborative approach, and EBSA is no
different. The best results happen when parents work as a team
with the school, mental-health-support providers and their child
to really listen and understand and collaboratively decide on an
action plan. The more the child feels heard and feels ownership
of the plan, the more likely it is to be successful. Baby steps are
usually far more effective than big leaps, but any move towards
re-attending school has to be at the pace of the child, with their
family and home seen as a safe space for them to be authentic
and able to co-regulate, in the same way that we discussed concerning restraint collapse (see page 140).

Choosing a school

If your child has yet to start school, you are in a fantastic position
because you can be informed right from the beginning about
how to help them and you can use your knowledge to choose
the best setting for them. Similarly, if your child is soon to make
the move to secondary or high school, knowing what to look for
will make for the easiest transition for you both.

So what should you look for in a school? To be honest, my
answer here would mostly be the same as if you were searching
for a school for a neurotypical child who had no behavioural
struggles. The first thing I would focus on is how nurturing the
school is. What is their approach to education and supporting
the holistic needs of children? How much time do children
have to get outside and move? What about a focus on creative
subjects, such as art or music? What are their school mottos and
rules? What are the beliefs about childhood and community
underpinning these? When you visit, how happy do the staff

seem? How happy and engaged are the children? Is a member of the senior-leadership team happy to meet with you to answer your questions and take you on a tour of the school on a regular day, outside of an open evening? (Only this will give a genuine view of the school.)

However, there are three specific things I would recommend that parents and carers of children with ADHD and co-existing conditions consider when choosing a school:

1. What is the school's behaviour policy? Is it an out-dated zero-tolerance, one-size-fits-all one that could be discriminatory for your child? Or does it have a more re-storative focus? All schools should make their behaviour policy available online, but if you can't find it, do email the school and ask them to send you a copy.
2. What is their SEND provision like? And what are the views and experience of the SENCo? (Ask to book a separate meeting with them to discuss how they would propose meeting your child's needs.)
3. Speak to other local parents of neurodivergent children who already have experience of the school. This will give you perhaps the most accurate information. Because it is all well and good having a well-designed website, a glossy brochure and salesy open evening, but it is only when you chat with those who have lived experience of the school that you get the real opinions. If you don't know anybody personally, find a local online discussion group for your area and ask parents of neurodivergent children to privately message you with their opinions.

Finally, I always recommend asking your child where they want to go. They may have different ideas to you, but trusting their instinct is incredibly powerful. This is something I don't think we do enough.

What if you are unhappy with the school?

Remember that you are your child's biggest advocate. But what does this look like when it comes to education? It means standing up for their rights, fighting for equity and reasonable adjustments for them, calling out the school when they have acted in a discriminatory way and being aware of your child's legal rights (see Resources, page 223 to help with this). What it doesn't mean, unfortunately, is being able to change every element of the school that you don't like.

It's impossible to find a school setting that agrees with every single belief and principle that you have. It doesn't matter if it's a state school, a private school or an alternative school – you are never, ever going to agree with everything that happens there. This is the harsh reality of our education system. But instead of trying to leap in and change everything that you're unhappy with, I'd recommend that you start with a focus on a few non-negotiables, or things that really matter to you and your child. For instance, you may not be happy for your child to miss their break time to be kept in for a detention because you know this makes their behaviour worse. This would be my starting point, letting smaller niggles go (at least for now, anyway). Compromise and focusing on the 'big stuff' is usually far more effective than constant complaints and attempts to revolutionise the school. There may well be many things that you dislike, but recognise that in a school setting it is just not possible to treat children in the same way that you would at home, not least because there are thirty other children to look after, but also because the way those children have been raised is all very different. Many will have been parented with mainstream rewards and punishment and the same approach will be expected at school.

With the way schools are understaffed and underfunded

at the time of writing, it's impossible to apply a truly bespoke approach to behaviour, affording each child the time and space that they need. This is deeply upsetting and infuriating, but it's the truth. As we discussed at the beginning of this chapter, the aims of school discipline are largely crowd control and making children as compliant as possible because of the pressures of government bodies and standardised testing. While I strongly disagree with this (in fact, I've written a whole book about it – it's called *Because I Said So!* if you're interested in learning more), it is a sad reality that will only change with a massive social movement and educational reform. Until then, I would suggest directing your ire at your local politician and trying to work with the school as much as possible. Frustratingly, you will not find a school that implements everything you like and nothing that you don't – the key is finding the one that is the best match to your child overall and one that you are 'happy enough' with.

Alongside this, recognise that the most important thing to understand is that you, at home, are the primary influence on your child. If you add up the number of hours a child spends at school versus at home (awake, that is), including holidays and weekends, they spend around 70 per cent of their waking hours with you. In other words, what you do at home with your child is significantly more influential than anything that happens at school. Especially when it comes to co-regulation and containment.

Finally, remember that teachers are struggling, too. I have not spoken to a teacher who doesn't wish there was more they could do to support children with SEND in their classes. Of course, there are some who are unsuited to the profession and should have left it a long time ago, but the majority I have met are kind, caring, passionate individuals doing their best in a system that is broken. Keep this in mind when you speak to them and raise your concerns. They are human, too, and working with them collaboratively will always bring the best results for your child.

This brings me to an important question: is school right for all children with ADHD? And indeed, is school the right place for your child? My answer to the first question is undoubtedly 'no'. Some children with ADHD and co-existing conditions thrive at school; some (like Flynn) will ultimately be happy there but have many struggles along the way; but for others, it is the most toxic place they can be. Some children need something different. Is school the right place for *your* child? Now that's a question I can't answer, only you – and they – can.

Alternatives to mainstream education

If you instinctively feel that school is wrong for your child, or perhaps you have tried it and you, and they, are struggling, what are your options? The answer here is not straightforward because it depends on where you live in the world. For this reason, I am going to concentrate this section on where I live in the UK. If you live elsewhere, please research the options in your location.

While you have several different choices for education in the UK, including alternative schooling such as Steiner and democratic schools, the two main ones are home education and something known as 'education otherwise than at school' (or EOTAS, for short). Let's take a quick look at each.

Home education

Home education looks different for everybody. Some people decide to follow a curriculum, planning out the day with specific lessons and timings, or follow an online school programme (often referred to as structured home education). Some people take a semi-structured approach, with a more formal focus on traditional academic subjects like mathematics (sometimes using a tutor for these) and a more free-range approach to others, including creative and artistic subjects. Finally, some base the education solely around their child's interests, taking an unstructured approach and letting the child take the lead with what, when and how they learn (this is often known as 'unschooling' or 'autonomous learning').

The term 'home education' can also be misleading, as much of the education happens in nature (sometimes embracing bush-craft and forest-school sessions) or while travelling the world (often known as world schooling), and some prefer to use home-ed co-operatives, where parents and carers share support, tuition, resources and expertise. The latter is very helpful for parents and carers who work full- or part-time outside of the home. The key to home education is understanding your child's interests and needs and balancing them with your own and your ability to support them. You absolutely do not have to have any teaching qualifications or expertise, just the willingness to learn with your child. If you worry about potential sensory overwhelm and needing to be with your child at all times (particularly if you struggled when you were thrown into involuntary home school-ing during Covid, which, incidentally, is nothing like conscious home education), this is precisely why co-operatives and local home-education communities are so important. Thankfully, there are thriving groups all around the country, providing friendship and support for children and parents/carers alike. If home education appeals to you, see the Resources section on page 223.

Education otherwise than at school (EOTAS)

EOTAS may, at first glance, seem to include home education (since it is, indeed, education that doesn't happen at school). However, it is very different. EOTAS is a special education package that is arranged (and importantly paid for) by the local authority when it becomes clear that school cannot meet the child's needs. EOTAS is, therefore, very different to elective home education, which is consciously chosen by parents and carers and their children.

Each local authority has an obligation to provide an education fit for a child who holds an Education, Health and Care Plan (EHCP) . If school cannot meet the child's needs, then the local authority must provide an alternative that can. This may be in the shape of home tuition, where a tutor visits your child at home or an agreed location outside of school for a specified number of sessions each week, often focusing on English and mathematics, online tuition with an online school or a tutor, or education held at another special provision centre. EOTAS can be helpful to children with ADHD and explosive behaviour who struggle to be in a school environment, but it does not provide the freedom or the ability to truly tailor the education to your child or give them the same autonomy as home education.

Here again, there is no singular 'best' option, but instead what will work best for your child and your family's circumstances. Giving your child a voice, however, is crucial. Similarly, if your child does leave mainstream education, giving them a period of time to decompress and regulate with no educational pressure, known as 'deschooling', is a wise choice, rather than rushing them straight into something else. Time to relax, recoup and regain their intrinsic passion for learning, which may have been destroyed by attending school, is key here.

What education do they really need?

A common question that parents ask when they are considering moving their child out of mainstream school is, 'But how will they do exams?' closely followed by, 'How will they get a job if they haven't done them?' The answer to both of these questions is simple: children educated at home, or 'otherwise than at school' can absolutely still take exams, such as GCSEs and A levels if you're in the UK. They can also progress into any further or higher education, training or career of their choice. The difference is that they will enter for the exams they want as an external candidate, rather than being entered for them en masse at school. The beauty here is that the children themselves can pick their interests and choose the subjects that appeal to them the most. Many will still take the standard mathematics and English exams (or in the UK sometimes 'functional skills', rather than the more in-depth GCSEs); some will take a whole array of ten or more different subjects; and some will instead pursue an alternative path. It is still possible to attend college or university if children are home educated, and while some may be home educated when younger, they may choose to attend a mainstream secondary school as they get older.

What children really need to thrive as they grow into adulthood is good mental health, self-esteem and confidence. Arguably, these are more important than any academic qualifications. Subjects such as budgeting, understanding household finances, cooking, gardening and growing food, home repairs, first aid and so on, which are key to success as an adult, are barely covered in school and are better learned at home anyway. Similarly, children with ADHD are often well suited to self-employment because of their natural tendency to entrepreneurship. Some of the best businesspeople in the world have few qualifications to their name, and an academic education cannot create the passion, flair, creativity and drive needed to succeed as an entrepreneur. Perhaps your child is not meant to work for others. Maybe their destiny is to create their own path. Once again, we are left with the analogy of fitting square pegs into round holes – this doesn't just apply to education, but to careers, too.

School often felt like a long, hard slog for Flynn and me, and in many ways, I feel it was the hardest part of raising a child with ADHD, because our education system is just not designed with the needs of neurodivergent children in mind. There were many times I felt that home education would have been better for us, and certainly easier. That said, those years certainly brought out my 'Mama Bear' instincts, and I learned an awful lot about myself. Flynn left school with a flurry of GCSEs and A levels and formed a good friendship group. Would I change anything if I could turn back the clock? I'm not sure. What I do know is that Flynn is happy and healthy and has a career that he enjoys – and that, ultimately, is the only thing that really matters. The route to the destination is, perhaps, less important.

Let's move on to our next chapter now, all about sleep and how it can look different for children with ADHD (and other co-existing conditions).

Chapter Seven

Sleep struggles

You may be wondering why there is a chapter about sleep in this book. After all, it is a book primarily about discipline and tackling explosive behaviour, so doesn't this chapter stick out a bit like a sore thumb? Night-time may be the one time that you get some respite as a parent and both you and your child can finally relax. At least that's the theory, anyway. The reality is that night-time can be just as difficult for children with ADHD and their families as the daytime, often more so. If nights make up between a third and a half of the time you spend with your child, the real question should perhaps be why do other books about ADHD only focus on behaviour in the daytime?

When I announced I was writing this book on my social media, I put a call out to my followers to ask them what they wanted me to cover. I expected their suggestions to focus on tackling explosive behaviour, navigating school, spotting co-existing conditions and juggling raising a neurodivergent child with being a neurodivergent parent. What I didn't expect, however, were multiple replies requesting sleep help. That said, the link between ADHD and sleep struggles is a strong one. Research has found that almost 67 per cent of adults with ADHD experience insomnia, compared with an average of 28 per cent of neurotypical adults.[1]

Studies questioning parents of children with ADHD, aged between five and eighteen, have found that up to half struggle with their child's sleep.[2] I must admit, I expected that figure to be higher and wonder if, like much research into neurotypical child sleep, parents may not always be aware of their child's wakefulness. Perhaps, too, given the popularity of infant sleep training in our society today, it is possible that these children have been trained to be quiet at night – that they are struggling, but their parents have no idea. Interestingly, given this point, much sleep advice for parents who have children with ADHD centres on the same old rewards and punishments: if the child goes to bed easily or stays in their room all night, give them a sticker; if they wake in the middle of the night, try to not make eye contact and avoid hugging them – instead, sit outside their bedroom door. These techniques are common, yet in the same way that they fail to consider the cause of the behaviour in the daytime, they also gloss over it at night. That said, it's clear that parents and carers and children alike do need help with sleep, but that help needs to look a little deeper, rather than simply masking the issues.

The negative cycle of sleep deprivation

Research shows that children with ADHD get between half an hour to an hour less sleep per night than their neurotypical peers of the same age.[3] They also experience more night wakings and more bedtime resistance. There is already much talk about how sleep deprived children (particularly adolescents) are today, with dire warnings about the consequences. For children with ADHD, these consequences are heightened. Sleep deprivation at night can cause them to feel tired in the daytime, especially at school, which can cause more problems with attention. It's no surprise that there is a direct link between poor sleep and lack of attention observed in educational settings.[4] A lack of sleep also causes children to be more aggressive and show more out-of-control and explosive behaviour, not just at school, but at home, too.[5]

Sleep deprivation doesn't just negatively impact children – it makes things much harder for exhausted parents who may find themselves getting frustrated and angry, more prone to harsh discipline and less able to help their children to co-regulate. What happens when parents are so tired they don't have the capacity to contain their child's tricky sleep and explosive behaviour? Everything gets worse. Daytime behaviour quickly becomes more out of control and the disconnect between parent and child worsens. In a desperately sad cycle, the very thing that these children need to help them to calm down is the one thing that they don't receive.

Research shows mothers of children with ADHD experiencing sleep problems have higher levels of depression than those with neurotypical children.[6] This makes perfect sense – combine the added exhaustion from broken nights and the lack of downtime with a society that is deeply unsupportive of mothers, in particular those of neurodivergent children, and you have a recipe for burnout. We'll talk much more about escaping this cycle in Chapter Ten, but for now, I'd like to focus on ways that parents and carers can improve their child's sleep, and not just palliate it with behaviourist-based sleep training.

Understanding common ADHD sleep challenges

The first thing I do when I work with parents struggling with their child's sleep is to help them to understand some basic sleep biology. It always shocks me when I read articles professing to solve your child's sleep problems that bypass this point. I find that even if nothing changes, helping parents and carers to understand their child's sleep a little more makes everything easier for them.

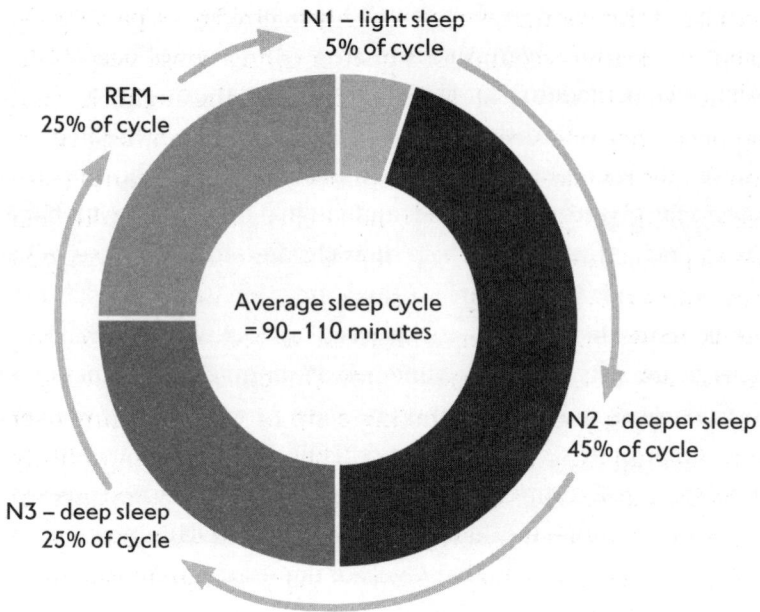

N1 – light sleep
5% of cycle

REM –
25% of cycle

N2 – deeper sleep
45% of cycle

N3 – deep sleep
25% of cycle

Average sleep cycle
= 90–110 minutes

The most important thing to understand about sleep is that nobody sleeps through the night. Everybody sleeps in cycles that usually connect with little to no awareness from the individual. Sleep cycles vary in length, depending upon age. A mature adult sleep cycle lasts for between 90 and 110 minutes. In babies, this is significantly shorter, but by the time a child has turned five, cycles are almost the same length as those of an adult. The cycle moves through two different types of sleep: REM (rapid eye movement) and NREM (non-rapid eye movement). NREM sleep accounts for about three-quarters of a sleep cycle, and is further subdivided into N1, N2 and N3. With the progression into each 'N' stage, sleep gets deeper. N3 is the deepest stage, often referred to as 'slow-wave sleep' (SWS), and it accounts for up to a quarter of the sleep cycle. After this, individuals enter into REM sleep, which is where dreaming occurs. REM sleep is not considered a restful sleep state because of the high levels of brain activity, but during this period the body is largely still due to a temporary loss of muscle tone.

Because of this contrast, it is commonly referred to as 'paradoxical sleep'. REM sleep accounts for a quarter of an average sleep cycle.

The issue in terms of 'sleeping through the night' is what happens once one sleep cycle ends and before another begins. Sometimes two sleep cycles can connect, with one running into the other. If this happens, you may believe that the individual has slept for three solid hours; if five sleep cycles connect, you may think they have slept for seven and a half hours. But you would be wrong. It is common to wake between sleep cycles. Think back to the last time you remember coming to at night and adjusting your pillow, taking a sip of water, turning over or pulling up the duvet or blanket. These things are most likely to happen after one sleep cycle has ended, just before another one starts. That's not to say that you don't ever wake during the middle of a cycle – you can and do – but you would likely need to be disturbed by something enough to wake you.

When children (and this includes teenagers) appear to wake regularly at night, it is likely that they are struggling to connect sleep cycles independently. This may be because of physical dis-comfort, or perhaps they do not feel adequately relaxed enough to sleep, or maybe they are anxious, or possibly, in the case of ADHD, their brains and bodies are buzzing too much. Of course, bribing them with a sticker, ignoring their cries, giving them a present if they 'sleep through the night' and don't call out for you or returning them back to their bed with as little eye contact as possible is not going to change any of this. All it does is to take away the containment and co-regulation that the child so desperately needs at a time when they are at their most vulner-able in an evolutionary sense – at night.

Rather than aiming for your child to 'sleep through the night', what you really want to happen is to help them to connect sleep cycles independently, to remove as many elements as possible that are preventing this from happening and to give them as many tools to use as you can.

Night waking isn't the only issue that parents and carers struggle with, however. Bedtime refusal and struggles with falling asleep top the list, too. How do you help these issues? My answer here is exactly the same: by finding the causes of the problems and helping the child to fix them.

Understanding sleep needs

I tend to find many parents and carers overestimate their child's sleep needs. This is understandable, given the stark warning messages about getting 'enough' sleep that schools so often share at the start of each new academic year and the way it is treated as a hot topic of conversation on television shows. But often, I find that parents and carers are scared into trying to get their child to sleep for longer than the child actually needs. When this happens – that is, if you're trying to get a child to sleep either before they are biologically ready or for longer than they need physiologically – you're going to be met with resistance, upset, anger and frustration. The key here is that when a child is wound up (and adults, too), they enter fight-or-flight mode, which sends cortisol coursing through their bodies and this, in turn, inhibits the hormone of sleep – melatonin. The child's brain and body senses threat and doesn't feel safe to relax and sleep, and any misguided attempts to try to cajole them to go to bed at what you presume is a reasonable time mean that they eventually fall asleep far later than you would like.

How much sleep does your child need? Here, it's important to understand that everybody is different. There is no one singular recommendation or a set number of hours based upon age. Instead, there is a recommended range.[7] Some children will sit right at the bottom of that range, needing very little sleep compared to their peers; some will sit right at the top and need a lot more than most. This range includes all sleep in a twenty-four-hour period, so if your child has a daytime nap, take this off the recommended range to give an indication of their need at night.

- Two years: 11–16 hours
- Three to five years: 10–13 hours
- Six to nine years: 9–11 hours
- Ten to twelve years: 9–11 hours
- Thirteen to eighteen years: 8–10 hours

Some children are OK with an hour less than these recommendations. For instance, some teens do perfectly well with only seven hours' sleep at night.

When it comes to the actual bedtime (i.e. the time that they get into bed to try to sleep), earlier is not always better. Once again, if a child is not physiologically ready to sleep, all that will happen if they go to bed early is that they will toss and turn and become frustrated that they can't sleep. And the more you try to get them to sleep early, the worse this will become. Finding the sweet spot for children is key here: we don't want them to go to bed too late, but too early is just as problematic. My suggested bedtimes (remember, here I mean the time of estimated sleep onset, not when you start the bedtime routine) are as follows:

- Two years: between 7 and 8 p.m.
- Three to five years: 8 p.m.
- Six to eight years: 8 p.m.
- Ten to twelve years: 9 p.m.
- Thirteen to eighteen years: 10 p.m.

Of course, if your child has an earlier bedtime and you are not concerned about their sleep, please don't change it. These recommendations are solely for parents and carers who worry about their child's sleep and struggle with bedtime resistance or night waking (or both).

Chronotypes

Perhaps you've heard of the terms 'night owls' and 'larks'? Or perhaps you call yourself 'a morning person' (or otherwise)? What you're referring to here is something known as a chronotype. Our chronotypes are like our own personal in-built clocks, driven by what is known as our circadian rhythm. Research has suggested that ADHD causes issues with our circadian time-keeping system.[8] There is an increased tendency towards 'eveningness' (or being a night owl), rather than 'morningness' (being a lark) in children and adolescents with ADHD. Children with ADHD are significantly more likely to need to stay up later at night and have a naturally later sleep onset than neurotypical children. Unsurprisingly, they also experience more daytime sleepiness and struggle to wake in the morning (if you have a teenager, I'm sure you've experienced this already). There is not much you can do about your child's chronotype in terms of changing it. However, being aware of it and, importantly, not fighting it by trying to aim for earlier bedtimes that your child is just not ready for are key to the easiest and calmest sleep for your whole family.

Restless legs syndrome and periodic limb movement syndrome

About a quarter of adults with ADHD have symptoms that mimic restless leg syndrome (RLS); in children, this can be as high as 40 per cent.[9] RLS is a neurological condition that makes the legs feel uncomfortable at rest, with an overwhelming urge to move them. RLS, understandably, makes sleep difficult. There is some research which shows that restless legs are linked with low iron levels in children, and so focusing on trying to encourage your child to eat iron-rich foods, or speaking to your family doctor about potentially taking an iron supplement, could help here.[10] Similarly, up to a quarter of children with ADHD struggle with something called periodic limb movement syndrome (PLMS), which causes their arms and legs to jerk uncontrollably, lasting from a few seconds up to a couple of minutes.[11] PLMS is also linked with an iron deficiency, so the same advice applies here. Some parents report success with using a magnesium cream or oil to massage the arms and legs before bedtime. PLMS may also co-exist with RLS.

Parasomnias

Parasomnias are a group of sleep disorders that includes unusual movements, perceptions and sensations, such as sleepwalking, sleep-talking and night terrors. Children with ADHD are significantly more likely to experience parasomnias than their neurotypical peers.[12]

The good news here is that most grow out of parasomnias naturally, but while you are waiting, your focus should be on keeping your child as safe as possible. There is some research showing that increasing levels of polyunsaturated fatty acids (PUFAs) in a child's diet can help to reduce parasomnias and improve sleep.[13] In one study, children were given 600mg per day of DHA (an omega-3 fatty acid) and actigraphy (a wearable electronic device) measurements of sleep showed an average of nearly an hour more per night.

Alternative ways to help your child's sleep

I need to begin this section with a huge caveat: many of the techniques recommended to help relax at bedtime are based on research with neurotypical children (or even adults) and can sometimes make things worse for children with ADHD. For instance, encouraging the use of meditation and mindfulness can be incredibly frustrating for individuals with ADHD who find it difficult to 'switch off' their brains. The recommended silence and darkness so often cited as 'good sleep hygiene' can be overwhelming, and some children with ADHD need more stimulation to relax and sleep, not less.

Please do not worry if I recommend something here that really does not work for your child. Just move on and try something different. My suggestions in the remainder of this chapter are just that – suggestions. They work for some and not others, and the last thing I want to do is to make things even harder for your child, or for you.

Take off the pressure

We have already discussed this briefly, but the pressure that is placed on children to unwind and go to sleep often makes things a lot worse. It is understandable from a parental perspective – you just want the best for your child and probably recognise that tiredness makes their behaviour worse. The trouble here is that the child can obsess about needing to sleep and, as they lie in bed, they become more attuned to their racing thoughts and their brains take a detour through every interaction they have had that day and often into obscure questions ('Which animal has the biggest brain?' 'Why do people like pineapple on pizza?'

and so forth), which then become a new hyper-fixation as they feel they must know the answer right now. Similarly, the focus on being awake while knowing they need to sleep is a great way to create stress and tension, guaranteeing that they will be awake for several more hours to come.

Depending on the age of your child, this may be a good time to have a discussion with them about the impact of psychological pressure on sleep and work, brainstorming ways that they can relax without focusing on their inability to sleep. My top two recommendations here are listening to audiobooks and reading because they focus the brain on something other than the onset of sleep.

Empty their container

Have you ever wondered why children open up to you at bedtime? Despite you asking them a million times 'How was your day?' or 'Are you OK?' in the evening. I find this very common with teenagers. I go to bed before my children these days, but I can't tell you how many times they've come into my room at midnight and said, 'Mum, are you awake?' and asked to talk. As much as I would rather roll over and say, 'Not now', I try my hardest to switch on my bedside lamp and say, 'Yes, what's up?' because bedtime is a perfect opportunity to allow children to empty their containers. Why does it happen then? Because you've finally stopped pressuring them to talk to you, and so they feel safe to offload at last.

If your child has had a difficult day, perhaps with lots of masking, or a tricky time at school because of their behaviour, then allowing them to empty their containers with you at bedtime is a great way to help them achieve better sleep, free of a whirring mind. If they are reluctant to open up to you, especially if they are a little older, then encourage them to write their thoughts down in a journal. This can be really helpful for those with rejection sensitive dysphoria, because pen and paper don't judge.

Co-regulation

I have worked for many years coaching parents about child sleep. One of the top issues I am asked to help with is how to get a child to go to sleep independently. If you watch any TV programme or film featuring a child going to bed, I can guarantee they will show a freshly pyjamaed child getting into bed, all smiles, with the parent snuggling their duvet or blankets around them. They may read them a quick bedtime story, then they will kiss them, turn off the bedroom light and walk out of the room. This is how society thinks it should happen, whether the child is one or ten. The thing is, this is not what a lot of children need.

Staying with your child, holding their hand, stroking their back or their forehead, or just sitting quietly on the floor or on a chair beside them as they go to sleep is a form of co-regulation. It's also a great way to encourage a speedier sleep onset. Don't be afraid to sit with your child or hug them to sleep, if it helps. You are not creating a rod for your own back or bad habits; you are co-regulating and, ultimately, building the skills for them to self-regulate, and get themselves off to sleep calmly, easily and independently in time.

Basic sleep hygiene

If you read any article or research study about child sleep, including those focusing on ADHD, the first thing they will usually recommend is good sleep hygiene. What does this mean? It means focusing on the sleep environment and the behaviour leading up to bedtime, such as a bedtime routine. Good sleep hygiene is the same for neurodivergent and neurotypical children – here are some tips:

- Keep the room as dimly lit as possible, with a small night light, if requested. Ideally, all lighting should be low blue light or red. Normal lighting (particularly white LED bulbs and anything blue in colour) has an inhibitory effect on the secretion of melatonin, the hormone of sleep. Some children will struggle with any lighting, however dim; in this case, using an eye mask (like the type you use on an aeroplane) can help to block everything out.
- Keep noises to a minimum, especially if they are distracting (like a ticking clock). Some children may prefer to wear soft earplugs to help block out all noises. You may want to play some relaxing 'alpha music' or white-noise soundscapes (which can help to relax and promote better sleep), although this is where my caveat comes in because some children with ADHD will really struggle with these, so do check your child's preference.
- Keep the room cool, if you can. It is harder to sleep in warm temperatures, again because warmth inhibits the secretion of melatonin (the body perceives it as sunlight or daytime). An ideal temperature is around 15–20°C. Opening a window to allow air to circulate can also help. It's best to have what I call a 'cool room, warm body': you don't want your child to be cold, but you do want the room to be cool.
- Set up a simple, calming bedtime routine that you repeat each night. For instance, start with a small bedtime snack and a cuddle, followed by a bath, shower or wash, toothbrushing, then into bed for a story or independent reading. It is the repetitive nature

of bedtime routines that make them so helpful, rather than the specific timings. If your child is younger, having a visual bedtime routine chart for them to follow (for instance, sticking pictures or photographs on the chart with Velcro after completing each segment) can really help.

- Try to avoid screens in the hour before bedtime and while going to sleep. I think we all know by now that screens are bad for sleep, and we have all heard the warnings about allowing children and teens access to screens in their bedrooms. However, I will add that for some neurodivergent individuals being able to watch a non-stimulating show can help them to drift off. If I'm struggling to sleep, I will pop something on Netflix and watch until I drift off. It's a classic case of taking the focus away from trying to sleep. If your child or teen finds this helps, make sure their device is set to 'night mode', with the screen brightness turned right down. For those who regulate by playing computer games in the run-up to bedtime I recommend getting them a pair of special blue-light-blocking glasses. These can be bought very cheaply and are very effective.

- Finally, the standard advice to avoid caffeine before bed doesn't tend to apply to younger children (simply because they rarely consume it). However, for teenagers you may be interested to learn that caffeine may help ADHD symptoms. A small dose of caffeine may have the same stimulatory impact on the brain as ADHD medication, which can induce a calming effect. So a small cup of milky coffee or sugar-free caffeinated drink shortly before bed may help your teen to sleep.[14] Of course, this may have the opposite effect, and if this is the case, it's definitely best to avoid caffeine from late afternoon onwards.

It's important to note that good sleep hygiene doesn't just apply to your child – it applies to you, too, especially as you are their role model. You can't tell your child to do one thing at night and expect them to accept it if you do the opposite.

Sensory needs

One area in which neurodivergent children may deviate from neurotypical ones when it comes to sleep is regarding sensory input, particularly if they have co-existing conditions such as sensory processing disorder or they are autistic. We have already covered some sensory aspects in this chapter, notably relating to sound and lighting, but there are several other small tweaks I suggest when I work with families:

- Switch to sleep sacks instead of duvets for restless sleepers who wake after getting twisted in their cover or kick it off during the night, then wake because of feeling cold. I recommend a special wadded sleepsuit with separate leg sections, allowing feet to be bare if preferred and enabling more movement than traditional sleeping bags. While these are more commonly used for babies and toddlers, you can find them in larger sizes, including some for adults.
- Check your child's pyjamas for any tags which may be itchy or irritate them and preferably unpick them, rather than cutting them out (the latter can leave an annoying little stub).
- Consider switching nightshirts to pyjamas if your child gets irritated with them riding up during the night. If your child prefers to have their legs bare, then pyjama shorts often work well.
- Consider switching bedsheets and nightwear to those

made from bamboo fibres, which are softer and crease less than traditional cotton ones. They also help with temperature regulation.

- Avoid pyjamas that have tight elastic around the wrists or ankles.
- Consider a weighted blanket if your child is five and older. The light pressure from the blanket can help them to feel calmer and more relaxed. For small children, however, this weight can compress chest movements and be unsafe for use overnight, so remove the blanket once they are asleep.
- Try a sensory cuddle cushion or a body pillow. These work in a similar way to weighted blankets, providing reassurance during the night and can be very helpful for children who need tactile stimulation at night.

There is no one right way to approach sensory elements of sleep – it's just whatever works for your child. Some children with ADHD will be helped by increasing sensory input at night, but others will need less to sleep well. Again, you know your child best.

Exercise

My family recently rehomed a rescue puppy. It quickly became apparent that he needed to move at night before he would sleep. Every night, between seven and eight o'clock, we have to play with him and get him moving. If we do this, he relaxes and drifts off to sleep easily; if we don't, then sleep is elusive. There have been many nights with him when I have thought how similar puppy parenting is to raising toddlers, and also older children who are prone to hyperactivity. We have to see their drive for movement as a need, not a want. Allowing them to get all their pent-up energy out, therefore, becomes an important precursor to the bedtime routine. Whether it's an after-dinner walk, some roughhousing, dancing in the kitchen or a quick kickaround in the garden or nearby park, it doesn't have to last for long – even ten minutes can make an enormous difference. Research shows a significant positive impact of pre-bedtime physical activity in children with ADHD, improving many aspects of sleep, including making it quicker for them to get to sleep, better overall sleep quality and fewer night wakings.[15]

The microbiome

According to research, having an atypical gut microbiome (the beneficial bacteria that live in our guts) can impact negatively on polyunsaturated-fatty-acid absorption and circadian rhythms in children with ADHD.[16] These can both negatively affect sleep. Focusing on foods that can improve your child's microbiome, such as a wide variety of fruit and vegetables and probiotics and fermented food, such as kefir and sauerkraut, can help here, or you may consider a child's probiotic supplement.

Medication timing and dosage

One of the side effects of most ADHD medication is insomnia. If your child is on medication and experiencing sleep difficulties, then I would recommend speaking to their consultant regarding changing their dosage, so that it provides maximum benefits in the daytime, but also allows them to sleep peacefully at night. Tinkering with the timing of taking tablets can help here, too – for instance, giving them to your child as soon as they wake in the morning, so that their impact on sleep has worn off at night.

What about melatonin?

Melatonin is a hormone secreted naturally by our bodies. Levels are at their highest at night, as our optic nerves and brains respond to a natural drop in both light levels and temperature. Individuals with ADHD can often have inhibited secretion of melatonin, meaning that their levels are lower at night than in neurotypical people. Many of the tips I have given so far in this chapter centre on helping children to relax, to allow their bodies to secrete more melatonin at night, encouraging their sleep naturally. In the UK, melatonin tablets or capsules are a prescription-only medication, and so you will need to visit your family doctor or your child's ADHD consultant to request them; in other countries, they can be bought from pharmacies without a prescription.

Research shows that melatonin supplementation is well tolerated and effective, producing improvements in sleep onset, sleep quality and reducing night wakes at dosages of 3–6mg per night; however, dosages as low as 1mg per night have also been shown to have a significant positive impact on sleep, with no safety concerns or lasting side effects, morning grogginess, gastrointestinal upset, dizziness and headache being the most common short-lasting ones.[17]

The decision to try melatonin has to be an individual one, in consultation with your child and, if you are in the UK, a relevant medical professional. For some children, taking exogenous (or external) melatonin tablets or capsules can be a game changer, with the benefits far outweighing any side effects. However, melatonin would always be the last thing I would turn to. Leaping straight into it without considering everything else I have mentioned in this chapter first runs the risk of using medication to mask underlying issues, which is never a good idea.

*

I know in my family, the days that followed extra late and disturbed nights were particularly hard for us all. It is all too easy to get into a negative spiral of poor sleep, leading to more explosive and difficult behaviour, then more anxiety and stress, which, in turn, creates more sleep problems. For this reason, sleep has always been something of a focus for me with Flynn, especially when he was still at school.

Sleep isn't only important to consider for children, but for adults, too. I've mentioned many times in this book how exhausting parenting is, and even more so if you are up against what often feels like the rest of the world, while trying to support your child and helping them to diffuse their behaviour. If you throw sleep deprivation into that mixture, too, then everything feels ten times harder. For this reason, I'd highly recommend you take a good, hard look at your own sleeping habits. Most of what we have discussed in this chapter applies to you, too.

Talking about focusing on your own sleep is a good point on which to close this chapter, as the remainder of the book turns all the attention on to you. We have focused a lot on your child so far in this book, but it is only when you consider your own behaviour and what you bring to the parent–child interaction that you slot in the last piece of the jigsaw and see the full picture.

Chapter Eight

Unmasking ourselves

I want to let you into a potentially uncomfortable secret: it is highly likely that you yourself are neurodivergent.

If you bought or borrowed this book to understand your own child, this chapter may come as a curveball or a bit of a rug-pull moment. Or maybe it won't be news to you at all. But as the parent of a child with ADHD (or suspected ADHD), the chance of you yourself having it, or a co-existing condition, is far more likely than not.

You know when people say, 'I think we're all a little ADHD' or 'Everybody is on the spectrum somewhere', it can sound so sensible in the moment – only it's not true, as we discussed in Chapter Two. You are either neurodivergent or you're not. You either have ADHD or you don't. There is no such thing as 'a little bit ADHD'. Having said that, as a parent of a child with ADHD, if you've ever thought, *Actually, some of the things mentioned in this book so far sound a little bit like me*, then I would wager you are almost definitely neurodivergent.

Do you remember in Chapter Two, when we were discussing the huge increase in ADHD diagnoses, and how many use this as a reason to explain why ADHD doesn't really exist? We discussed that the age group most likely to receive a diagnosis is not children, but adults. This isn't because adults are somehow just developing ADHD, but rather that they have always had it. They just didn't realise.

If you are a child of the 70s, 80s or 90s you probably grew up in a very different world. One where neurodivergence was rarely mentioned, children with ADHD were just 'the naughty ones' or 'the weird ones' and where the most exposure you had to autism was the film *Rain Man* (which, incidentally, contains many damaging stereotypes). If you struggled with anxiety, you were probably taught to 'suck it up'. If you had sensory difficulties, you were likely told to 'stop being so sensitive' and any emotional dysregulation was probably ignored, chastised, ridiculed or punished. As a result, you most likely learned to live inauthentically, and slowly built a mask to hide behind, both with your own family and out in wider society.

You've probably got pretty good at playing the role of a neuro-typical person by now, but maybe you have the odd moment of wondering if you're different or questioning why other people seem to be more confident, calmer, tidier or more able to cope with the demands of everyday life than you. Maybe you sub-consciously see elements of yourself in your child's behaviour, which trigger you, and so you desperately want better for them, and of them, than you experienced. This last point is especially difficult if you're the parent of a child or children with ADHD, particularly when you add your own dysregulated behaviour into the picture, too – because the pressure it places on all of you can be overwhelming.

Our children hold up a mirror to us

Every single parenting book I have written (this is number six-teen, if you're interested) has placed an emphasis on changing parental behaviour in order to change the child's. But the focus in Western society, with parenting TV programmes akin to dog-training ones, is to produce a quick-fix change to a child's behaviour, and this approach is ineffective, at least in the long term. Techniques such as reward charts, lots of praise, naughty steps and time out may produce superficial changes in behaviour quickly, but as soon as the expert leaves the family's home, the effects will start to wane. The lack of a long-term impact is largely because the person who needs to do all the changing is the parent, not the child. Whether I'm writing about child sleep, eating, tantrums, potty training or teen defiance and sibling arguments, the key is educating parents and helping them to change their beliefs, expectations and their own behaviour. Only then does lasting change happen.

When you have a child with ADHD, you quickly realise that conventional discipline techniques don't work (as we discussed in Chapters Four and Five), and that you have to find another way. The alternative needs to start with taking a long, good look at ourselves. We realise that our children will do as we do, not as we say, and if we want them to be calm and regulated, we will never achieve that through yelling, punishment, consequences and adding our own dysregulation into the mix. Our children do a great job of reflecting our own behaviour back at us, especially when they – and we – are neurodivergent. This is why this chapter is so important – because to understand your child, you have to start with understanding yourself and the impact you may be having on them.

If you have been ignoring a large part of yourself for most of your life, it is impossible to consider your reflection unless you peel back the mask. I know this is hard, but as much as you may want a quick and easy fix for your child's behaviour, this is necessary work, not only to help them, but to help the child within you, too. Later in this chapter, we'll hear from some parents about how they realised they themselves were neurodivergent, and how they balance this with their child's ADHD (and other co-existing conditions), while in Chapter Ten we will talk in depth about balancing everybody's needs, including your own, particularly when parenting feels impossible. But for now, I'd like to tell you about my own journey to unmasking myself.

My story

The best way I can describe my childhood is by saying I felt like I was on the periphery, looking in at others enjoying themselves and appearing to find everything much easier than I did. That's not to say that I wasn't happy. I was. I had a happy home life and also had friends – a small, select handful who I remain close to to this day – but I always felt more comfortable being alone. Socialising has always been deeply uncomfortable for me. I have never understood small talk, I struggle with the timing of conversations and knowing when I should speak. I either stay completely silent or end up blurting something out and speaking over others. My family called me a 'shy' child and tried to encourage me to be less socially awkward, but this only made me more anxious and more aware of my awkwardness around others. I have always found social situations incredibly draining, so much so that now, as an adult, I book in alone time to decompress the day after I have to be out in public, otherwise I reach burnout very quickly. I thought this was all normal.

I would spend hours counting objects as a child (I still do, actually). If we went on a car journey, I had to count every single lamppost and read every car number plate. It wasn't an activity I chose to occupy me; it was something I had to do, a compulsion I couldn't ignore. I simply couldn't not do it. I would also often get 'stuck' doing something, whether that was counting shapes in our wallpaper, or pressing each button on our leather Chesterfield sofa – again, this didn't feel like something that was under my conscious control. I was a good student at school, never getting into trouble, but my school reports always mentioned my daydreaming and lack of focus and not engaging in the class. On weekends, I would spend hours organising my collection of sugar packets (the small ones you often get in coffee shops) in scrapbooks. I collected them wherever I went. I thought this was all normal.

As a child, I had huge sensory issues. I couldn't wear wool, or polo necks, or stiff or heavy clothing, and I couldn't abide having my hair brushed. I still cannot walk on carpet barefoot, be in the same room as somebody brushing their teeth, wear jeans, tight-fitting socks, a coat or a watch for more than an hour or two. Certain sounds, particularly my father eating, made me feel an intense rage, and I have always seen patterns and colours for days of the week and months of the year. I thought this was all normal.

As I got older and started work, I developed terrible imposter syndrome and anxiety. I constantly worried about what people thought of me and would spend hours replaying conversations in my head each day. If I had to go somewhere new, I would pore over a map for hours, planning my route and timings with precision. The dawn of Google Streetview was a revelation – now I always 'walk' my routes virtually before setting off. When I go on holiday, I print out an in-depth daily itinerary, running into tens of pages, always stored in the same black plastic folder. My family tease me for it, but I cannot enjoy a holiday without it. When I go to the gym, I have to use the same locker and changing room and shower cubicle; as I walk in, I will them to be empty, and if they're not, my gym session will start with me feeling discombobulated when I have to find an alternative. I thought this was all normal.

I thought everybody else struggled with these things, that this was the standard human experience, but that others just coped better than me. I realise now that everything I've learned about social situations, I have learned by observing people. People-watching and body-language observation became something I was an expert in. I would assess my response in a social situation, compare it to others' and then tweak my responses next time. I tried on the personalities and mannerisms of those I respected and built a persona that I was finally happy with. It felt inauthentic and tiring, but everybody acts out a character in public, don't they? I thought this was all normal.

It has only been in the last couple of years that I've realised the intense effort it takes me to be in social situations is not normal. Neither are my sensory issues. Or my intense need for order and routine. I began to strongly suspect that I was neurodivergent, and when I learned that ADHD was hereditary, everything finally began to make sense. I have never sought a diagnosis. I wrangled with the idea of getting one, but I'm not sure I feel the need now as an adult, though I understand it validates others hugely. I think the decision on whether to seek a diagnosis for yourself as an adult is a deeply personal one.

I have done a lot of research and reading and have taken every self-test I can find. I score highly on autism tests, such as the Autism Spectrum Quotient (AQ) with a score of 38 out of 50 (the cut-off for an autism diagnosis is 29, and the average score of a neurotypical person is 16).[1] Like any self-test, there are issues with this questionnaire – some questions seem outdated and not a true reflection of autism, and there is not much nuance. Self-testing can also be unreliable because of subconscious bias. One area of the AQ questionnaire that is sorely lacking is the concept of masking, particularly in women. I know I have learned how to act in social situations from people-watching, and I can put these learned skills into action, but they never feel natural; the AQ test, however, does not consider masking. The Camouflaging Autistic Traits Questionnaire (the CAT-Q) is specifically designed to test for autistic camouflaging traits.[2] In this one I score 155 (a score of over 100 is indicative of autistic masking, with the average autistic female scoring 124 and the average neurotypical female scoring 90).

I strongly suspect that I am at least autistic and have synaesthesia and misophonia (see page 34). I also wonder if I may have inattentive-type ADHD. Interestingly, I am also hypermobile, a condition we learned in Chapter One is strongly associated with neurodivergence. I am also pretty sure that my late father had ADHD. He was constantly moving, always bored and trying to find something to occupy himself. As a child, he struggled lots at school with his behaviour and had quite a severe stammer. It seems the neurodivergent genes are strong in my family!

I often wonder how my childhood, adolescence and adulthood up until now would have been different if I had understood that others didn't all experience life as I did. If I had realised that every struggle I thought was normal actually wasn't. What would have been different if I had given myself grace for the things that I found so hard? I catch myself thinking about 'little Sarah' and wishing I could go back in time to let her know that she was never the problem. I think perhaps this is why I'm so passionate about being respectful to children today and why it has become almost my life's purpose. Or perhaps I should say my hyper-focus?

ADHD in women – the hidden, misdiagnosed and misunderstood

As we have discussed several times in this book already, many neurodivergent adults are living without a diagnosis. Perhaps, like me for many years, they have no idea that they are autistic or have ADHD, or perhaps they have an inkling that they are different to others but are not sure what to do about it. While boys are more likely to be diagnosed in childhood (particularly those displaying hyperactive behaviour), girls often grow into adulthood with no diagnosis, or indeed suspicions that they are neurodivergent. It's not until they are reaching midlife that the pieces start to fall into place. In fact, most women with ADHD are not diagnosed until they are in their thirties or forties. Isn't that shocking? So many little girls, teenagers, young women and new mothers struggling through life, thinking that they are the problem and blaming themselves for not being 'good enough' unnecessarily. So many being incorrectly diagnosed with depression, anxiety, exhaustion and other mental-health disorders, when the underlying root cause – their ADHD – was missed. It makes me so angry to think about how many of us have been let down. It is only in the last decade that researchers have begun to explore the long-term effects of ADHD as girls grow into women; as with many things in our patriarchal society, it is the women who are overlooked.[3]

What can undiagnosed ADHD look like in women? First, we have to consider how most learn to mask their symptoms – how, over decades, they learn to hone their camouflage, often becoming master chameleons. Many women with ADHD will have been stereotypical 'good girls' in childhood. By this I mean they would have tried to keep their emotions to themselves if they thought their parents needed them to be 'good' and not cause them too much bother. Sometimes this happens because parents are stressed, busy at work, having relationship or health issues, or perhaps they were struggling with their own neuro-divergence and emotion regulation. These girls learn to bury their feelings and needs so as not to add any extra mental load on to their parents; they also learn that when they are quiet and 'good', with few needs, their parents are more regulated and calm around them. The problem here is that the good girl grows into adolescence and adulthood learning to internalise her feelings and hiding her needs to keep everybody around her happy. Then, when she becomes a mother, she prioritises her family above herself – she has spent years learning how to camouflage and fit into the world and she becomes good at juggling the mental and practical load of parenting, too, because she has to. All this masking and ignoring her own needs, however, stretches her so thin that at some point she snaps. When her mask slips, she may reach a period of intense burnout or low mental or physical health (sometimes both). Decades of living inauthentically can leave her with severe anxiety or depression, and she may struggle with perfectionism, or imposter syndrome, forever trying to meet the unrealistic expectations she holds for herself. Sometimes the rejection sensitive dysphoria is so severe that she may question if she is a failure and think everybody hates her, including her children.

So many women display red flags that are missed for decades, and when you really open your eyes and see them, you wonder how anybody could have overlooked them. Alas, we live in a misogynistic and sexist society that still labels young girls as 'overly sensitive' if they struggle with their emotions, or 'tomboys' if they are energetic. We commonly blame mental-health struggles on female hormones – for instance, 'stroppy' teenage girls going through puberty and 'cantankerous' or 'scatty' middle-aged women going through the menopause. ADHD is still wrongly seen as a 'boy issue', and hundreds of thousands of women have been let down as a result.

If you are female and you identify with anything I've written in this section, please consider seeking a diagnosis. You were never the problem – the world that you live in is.

Healing your neurodivergent inner child

Realising that you are neurodivergent later in life can be incredibly validating and freeing. It can also leave you with a feeling of bereavement, and it is common to feel the need to grieve the life that might have been. What would have been different if people had understood you? What things would they have said, or perhaps more importantly would they not have said, if you had known about your neurodivergence from an early age? Would school have been different for you? Friendships? Relationships? Your career? What about the early years of parenting, when you were transitioning through matrescence (the metamorphosis of early motherhood). So many things could have been different if only somebody had picked up on your neurodivergence.

I am a big advocate of focusing on the moment and what you can change, rather than what you can't. But I also feel that allowing yourself to grieve is important. Perhaps you have come across the five stages of grief before? Introduced by psychiatrist Elisabeth Kübler-Ross in 1969, these stages are used predominantly to explain the mourning process and the feelings that those with a terminal illness experience, but they are also pertinent to any situation that involves a sense of grief, which I feel is incredibly relevant to being able to move on after realising, as an adult, that you are neurodivergent.[4] The stages are: denial, anger, bargaining, depression and acceptance.

1. Denial

The first stage is a defence mechanism, where the individual will dismiss and deny what is happening. In this case, self-talk such as, 'This is silly, I'm not neurodivergent. I was just a difficult child,' is common.

2. Anger

This anger may be self-directed or, more commonly, directed at others, such as your parents or teachers, asking yourself, 'Why didn't they notice I was struggling so much?' You may also feel increasingly irritable and short-tempered with these people, or just in general.

3. Bargaining

This stage of grief often involves making bargains with higher powers, such as praying to a religious deity and asking for another chance. In the case of grieving about your neurodivergence, you may find yourself asking 'What if?' a lot and thinking about things you, or others, could have done, or said, to have brought about a different outcome.

4. Depression

The fourth stage of grief is one that is perhaps the most recognisable, as denial, anger and bargaining give way to sadness, a loss of interest in the things that once gave you pleasure and changes to your eating and sleep habits. While it may feel as if this phase will never end, recognising that you are towards the end of the grief cycle is key.

5. Acceptance

The final phase sees individuals coming to terms with their situation, accepting what has happened and learning to move on, whether that is forgiving themselves or, often, forgiving their parents and carers. Regarding the acceptance stage, one very important point to understand is the fact that if you are neurodivergent, it is highly likely that one or both of your parents is, too. If they are not diagnosed, the dissonance, denial and masking that they have experienced for their whole life has likely impacted on their inability to recognise your struggles. Once you realise this, I find it becomes a lot easier to be able to forgive and move on.

EXERCISE: WRITE A LETTER TO YOUR INNER CHILD

A powerful technique I use often with parents who are struggling with something that happened to them during their own childhood, especially if it is preventing them from being able to support their child well in the present, is to write themselves a letter.

First, find a photograph of yourself as a child, if possible at the age you feel you most struggled at. Take a minute or two to look at the picture and remember how you felt at that age. What did you find particularly difficult? What was your self-talk like? What were your fears? Or worries? Now, take a piece of paper and a pen, or use an electronic device, and write a letter to the younger you. What do you wish somebody had told you back then? What words would have helped you to understand yourself better? What support do you wish you had received? Maybe your letter will be an apology to your younger self for what you went through un-necessarily. Or perhaps it will be a list of affirmations, telling yourself how brave you were, or pointing out all the positive traits that were so often overlooked. Perhaps your letter will be more like a diary entry, noting down how you felt as a child, and then reflecting on those feelings as an adult. There is no one right way to do this – just write whatever comes into your head. Or if writing feels too difficult, you could record a voice note.

When you have finished, you have the option to keep the note or destroy it. Some people feel a release by burning a physical piece of paper or deleting each word on their electronic device. Others prefer to keep the notes saved, to come back to and reflect on in the future. Whatever feels the most helpful for you is best.

Being a neurodivergent parent

Realising that you yourself may be neurodivergent doesn't just help you to come to terms with your past, it can also help you with your parenting in the present. All parents make mistakes; and all parents question their parenting abilities at times. When you are a neurodivergent parent of a child with ADHD, however, the challenges you face are usually far and above those faced by neurotypical parents of neurotypical or even neurodivergent children. I find the most common difficulties include:

- struggling to play with your children, especially imaginary or unstructured play
- difficulties with constant noise from your children
- feeling overwhelmed by the needs of your children and the everyday demands of parenting
- feeling touched out, in particular with young children who need you to hug them to sleep every night
- needing time alone to decompress, often at the times when your children need you most
- sensory overload from the constant movement of your children
- your child's almost constant need for entertainment and dealing with their boredom
- the general demands of 'adulting' and having to organise everything, especially when children start school and a million letters are sent home, and when your child struggles to remember things that they need
- the morning rush to leave the house on time
- feeling like your head will explode from holding so many thoughts and to-do lists at once
- rejection sensitive dysphoria when you make a

parenting mistake and worry that your child will hate you, or that you have damaged them for ever.

Of course, this list barely scratches the surface, and I don't have any magic solutions, I'm afraid (but once again, Chapter Ten is all about balancing your needs and feelings as a parent). I hope that recognising the extra challenges you face will help you to be a little kinder to yourself, though. Life feels hard right now because it *is* hard, not because you are not a good parent. Showing yourself grace, acceptance and patience is so important.

I wanted to end this chapter with some quotes from some neurodivergent parents of children with ADHD or explosive behaviour. Maybe they will resonate as much with you as they did with me.

'It has been a journey for me and I have had to do some painful reflection on my own tendencies towards rigidity and black and white thinking, which took the form of believing there was one single and "right" way to parent. I have come to understand that, in fact, a key part of being a parent is working out what is the best approach for my own unique child and admitting that I may have been wrong in the past.'

'Having ADHD as a parent can feel like you're going in slow motion. There are a hundred million things whizzing around in your mind and no clarity to any of these thoughts whatsoever. Outwardly, it's paralysis. Inside, it's a barrage. Like trying to push through a force field. Then an outburst from your child can cut through it all and bring a new perspective. A panicky, jittery, breath-stealing perspective. Why isn't Mummy paying attention? Why won't she answer me? *I'm here, my love. Holding down the frantic and trying to appear calm. I'm here. I'm in here, somewhere.*'

'Becoming a parent induced a new level of anxiety, because it meant, among other things, that I couldn't exert all of my energy on masking. It made me more vulnerable than ever. I think back to the sheer doom I felt when the reality of motherhood dawned on me and I laugh, because little did I know. I thought it would be hard, but the worst-case scenario I imagined still isn't as hard as it is on a daily basis. The juggling is insane. Key moments foggy, then panic-stricken. It's impossible. We do it, but it's impossible.'

'I find it almost impossible to relax. Even before having my daughter, I always felt I had a huge running to-do list and my mind was constantly dealing with racing thoughts, which is very exhausting. This affects my ability to get restful sleep, too. I suffer from rejection sensitive dysphoria, where the slightest thing can cause me to feel almost immediately dejected, such as being left on read or misinterpreting somebody's reaction to me. I really struggle with overthinking.'

'Picture a busy house: the radio is on in the kitchen, the TV is on in the lounge, the tumble dryer is whirring away, the extractor fan is on, the pot of boiling water on the stove bubbles over, one child pulls on my sleeve, the other passes me a book and my poor, darling husband asks me a question and I flip my lid. "What do you mean what's for dinner? If you made it once in a while, then maybe you'd know!" Cue everyone staring, bamboozled at my rage, as that rage turns to sadness and then shame. Days like this can lead to burnout, when my tired is tired and my motivation has left the building. I don't want to socialise, I don't want to do anything, my self-esteem is in tatters and I feel like the worst human in existence. Why can't I just get on with it like everyone else? It's pathetic, I'll tell myself. Until I've had a rest and then I'll be much kinder to myself.'

'When I am dysregulated, it is often because of layers of sound. I can enjoy one sound very loudly, like rock music, but when a child is crying, a pan is boiling, my husband is talking, my five-year-old is asking me questions and the doorbell goes, it feels like the world is closing in and my stress levels skyrocket. I struggle to think and feel like my skin is on fire. I just need all the conflicting sounds to stop immediately, so I can calm down. I wish I had known about this overstimulation as a child, and I wish my parents had known to give me a tight hug and make some of the noises stop. Just a calm face, gently sat next to me, inviting me into a tight hug would have been a game changer.'

'Discovering I had ADHD in my thirties has helped me accept what I saw as my flaws. The continuous losing my car keys, leaving the keys in the front door, forgetting appointments. My brain is like I've got twenty tabs open; sometimes I don't know where to start or what to prioritise. The coping strategies I have can make me come across as rigid, obsessive, demanding or difficult. In order to be able to stay on track I have daily routines and become very angry when I'm not able to complete my tasks. My impulsivity is a blessing and a curse. I am not good with money; luckily my husband is and managed the finances. My compulsive spending is something I've worked hard on to question myself, why am I buying this? Which has then taken me the other way and I put off buying things I or my children need out of fear I'm wasting money. However, I am good at coming up with in-the-moment ideas and thinking quickly on my feet. As a mum of two young children my ADHD has pros and cons. I have a very strong drive, which is helpful in terms of getting things done, but sometimes it takes over and means I'm missing out on spending time with my family because "I just have to get this done". My emotional regulation is challenging, especially when I am on my period.

I then feel like a terrible mum for snapping at my children and not demonstrating the patience and compassion I try so hard to show them. My rage and outbursts can be very hard to control and I then feel deep shame after overreacting.'

'Since becoming a parent I feel like my masking skills have been depleted. I'm exhausted when I'm home with my children, a mental and emotional exhaustion.'

I hope that you have found this chapter helpful, especially considering that this book is supposed to be about your child, and not about you. I find that the most important step towards healing as a family when a child has ADHD or explosive behaviour is to really understand the perspective of each family member, the triggers and demons they may bring and the interplay between all these. Certainly, making peace with my own past has helped me to be a better mother in the present, and letting go of some of the heavy baggage that I was carrying has made me a calmer person in general.

As a parent, you are the key to dealing with your child's challenging behaviour. Everything starts with you, even (and especially) when it doesn't feel like it. That may sound like I'm blaming you for your child's behaviour, but I promise I'm not. In fact, the next chapter is all about accepting the fact that *none* of this is your fault.

Chapter Nine

It's not your fault

It was all my fault. I was a terrible mother. Perhaps it was the time I left him to cry because I was too exhausted to pick him up again. Or perhaps it was the time I shouted at him as a toddler when he went to pull the cat's tail. Maybe it was because I gave him formula milk or jarred baby food and didn't feed him 100 per cent home-prepared, completely organic food, like I did his brother. Maybe it was because I had had an epidural during labour. Maybe it was because my labour was induced. Maybe I didn't read to him enough or play with him enough. Maybe I didn't cuddle him enough because I was busy running around after his toddler brother. Maybe I wasn't strict enough. Maybe I was too strict. It was my fault. It had to be. Everybody says that children are poorly behaved because of lax parenting and here was the result of mine ...

Maybe you identify with some of these thoughts? I'm pretty certain you've had similar. When you're the parent of a child with ADHD or undiagnosed explosive behaviour, you spend a lot of time searching for answers, reasons, causes and failures. You're constantly looking for things you did wrong, or things that you didn't do that you should have done. Once you accept that it's not your child's fault, it's natural that your thoughts turn to yourself as the next suspect. The irony is that you're reading a book about how to understand and be a supportive parent to your child. If you were really a bad parent, you wouldn't be doing that, would you? But it probably doesn't matter what I say, because you've likely been so tough on yourself that you've started to believe your own self-doubts and attacks.

The entirety of this chapter is in this book for one reason: to help you realise that *it's not your fault*. It never was. And now, it's time finally to stop blaming yourself.

Why *do* we apportion blame to ourselves so much as parents? I think, in part, it's a sign of good parenting – the fact that you want to learn and improve and think critically about your actions. The intense blame, however, takes this introspection a step too far. I also think it stems from society and the way that parents of children with explosive behaviour are treated.

Let's take a look at some of the specific causes of parental guilt when your child has explosive behaviour.

The refrigerator mother

In 1943, psychiatrist Leo Kanner published a paper on early infantile autism. Kanner recognised the hereditary aspect of autism in that he noted how some families displayed similar autistic behaviours. He also referred to autism as something that is innate (or 'born with') and believed it to be rare. Despite this, Kanner also indicated that he believed parents, particularly mothers, contributed to the condition through emotionally cold parenting.

In the 1960s, Bruno Bettelheim, an Austrian psychologist influenced by Kanner's work, stated that he felt the cause of autism was 'the refrigerator mother', or a mother who frequently displayed coldness towards her child. Mother blaming was rife at the time (even worse than it is today) and Bettelheim's proclamations became a view held by much of society. The idea that mothers who are unable to be emotionally warm with their children were the major cause of autism has thankfully long since been discredited; however, the repercussions of the theory live on in society today. Ironically, while some undoubtedly still believe that autism and ADHD, alongside other behavioural difficulties, are linked with an absence of maternal warmth, many now also blame mothers for being too nurturing and not strict enough. Basically, we can't win. These theories indicate that there is some sort of sweet spot – not too cold, but not too warm either, an emotional and maternal optimal thermostat of sorts – and if we don't hit the right temperature, then it's our fault our children behave the way they do. Is it any wonder so many of us blame ourselves?

Sexism and traditional parenting roles

There is a strong chance that if you're reading this book, you are female. I don't say that to stereotype men and women, fathers and mothers – it is simply a reality and one that I wish wasn't true. My own social media followers are 98 per cent female. Parenting books are predominantly bought and read by women (and, indeed, written by them). I desperately want to see this change (and there are some amazingly involved fathers; perhaps you're one of them?), but the emotional work and thinking of parenting is still seen by society as a role that is fulfilled mostly by mothers. When you combine this with the pressure on women to work full-time, as well as parenting as if they don't have a job, you end up with many exhausted women who feel that they are failing. There is also an interesting difference in the psychology of men and women when it comes to them (suppos-edly) not doing a job well: men tend to externalise and look for outside reasons why they couldn't succeed, or they blame bad luck; women, on the other hand, tend to look inwards and blame themselves.[1] When you consider this internalising propensity and the societal pressure to be 'a good mother' (alongside juggling a million life balls), it's no wonder that so many mothers of children with ADHD and explosive behaviour consider that it's their fault. That's not to say that fathers do not feel similarly – just that the number feeling that way is on a far smaller scale.

Parenting-course recommendations

If a child is out of control, it must be because of the parents. That's the message television parenting shows usually give us. A childless nanny quickly sweeps in, tells off the parents as much, if not more so than the children and leaves everybody scared and subdued into behaving better. On a superficial level, I can understand why professionals such as doctors, child psychiatrists and psychologists and teachers believe that the child's behaviour is ultimately a product of poor parenting. When I work with parents, most of what I suggest is, indeed, about changing their own behaviour in order to see a change in their child's. What I have issue with, however, is the compulsory demand that parents seeking a diagnosis for their child's behaviour must be made to take a parenting course before the diagnostic process commences. They may as well just say, 'We actually think you are the problem, and we want you to learn how to parent properly before we even consider your child being neurodivergent.' This undermines parental instincts, self-belief and confidence and, ironically, a parent who is doubting and blaming themselves for everything is one who is going to find themselves struggling to regulate their own emotions and be more likely to act in a dysregulated way with their children.

Is everybody a great parent? No, of course not. But the idea that all parents of children with ADHD or explosive behaviour seeking help and a diagnosis are bad parents is ridiculous beyond belief. Add to this many of the courses parents are forced to attend are horrendously outdated and fixate on behaviourist methods that are ineffective and unsuitable for neurodivergent children.

When I was trying to seek a diagnosis for my son, I came across this ridiculous hurdle. I was told that we couldn't be referred for a specialist paediatrician appointment unless my husband and I had completed a parenting course. At this point I had written five parenting books, had taught thousands of parents via workshops, trained hundreds of professionals and launched a multinational parenting-class company with over a hundred practitioners trained under me. I tried to explain all of this, but I was met with blank stares and 'unfortunately-we-can't-skip-this-step' remarks. We finally agreed on a mind-boggling compromise: they were satisfied if I took my own course that *I* had written and designed with a practitioner *I* had trained. I had never heard anything so ludicrous in my life. I printed myself off a certificate of attendance, signed it myself (as the director of the training company) and gave it in. It was accepted and our referral finally progressed.

When we force parents seeking help to take a parenting class, we undermine their confidence and we just add another string to the 'it's my fault' bow. Perhaps we haven't moved on so much from the refrigerator-mother theory, after all?

So-called cures advertised to parents

Perhaps you've seen adverts on social media advertising for dietary supplements, herbal medicines, specific diet plans, alternative-therapy treatments, bodywork sessions, educational and meditation apps all claiming to either 'cure' ADHD or radically reduce the symptoms? The way that social media algorithms work means that parents of children with ADHD or explosive behaviour are served adverts related to videos they watch, groups they are members of or links they click on, and you can very quickly find yourself inundated with these, all claiming to change your child's life (and yours). The problem here (aside from a lack of honesty and ethics) is that they all come with a steep price tag. In the midst of a cost-of-living crisis, when we're all working hard to keep a roof over our children's heads and food on the table, these sorts of expensive so-called 'cures' are out of budget for most. And what happens when you think that there is a treatment out there, but you can't afford it for your child? It adds another tick on the 'it's-my-fault' list. If only you were rich enough, you could help your child. It's your fault you're not. Of course, it isn't – not even remotely – but that doesn't stop the guilt you carry from getting ever heavier.

The uninformed beliefs of others

There is so much stigma in our society around ADHD and children with explosive behaviour. Far too many people think that ADHD doesn't really exist and is just an excuse for 'bad behaviour' and many, particularly those from older generations, believe that dysregulated behaviour in children is a direct reflection of parenting ability. One research study looking at mothers of four- to ten-year-olds with disruptive behaviour found that almost 40 per cent of them felt stigmatised by others, mostly family members, schools and their social network.[2] To be honest, I'm surprised this number is so low, I would have placed it far nearer to 100 per cent.

When we feel that others are judging us and our parenting abilities, we tend to internalise these beliefs and start to believe their words. This stigmatisation is commonly linked to mothers isolating themselves from other adults, which only compounds their fears and worries, as they are left to ruminate on them alone. Interestingly, the research also found that mothers who felt stigmatised tended to seek a diagnosis for their children earlier than those who didn't. This feels like an indicator that they are caring and heavily invested in their children's wellbeing to me – a far cry from negligent parenting.

For me, one of the hardest parts of being a mother to 'that child' was the whispers and sideways glances at the school gate. It would be nice to think I was being paranoid, but some of the other parents chose to speak at full volume, with no attempt to disguise their views. I'm sure you know the sorts of passive-aggressive parents I mean – those who would be sickly sweet to your face, but if there were any remaining doubt about their feelings towards your family, the lack of party invitations for your child cemented their view. They do not want their child anywhere near yours. In these painful and lonely moments, I defy any parent to not blame themselves and consider that everything is their fault. Now and again, I see the mothers who whispered about my child and me in the school playground and I have to fight an urge to go up to them and tell them that my child finally received a diagnosis and that their words hurt us both unimaginably. I also take a sort of twisted pleasure in learning that my child is in a much better place now, career- and life-wise, than theirs. But in my more rational moments, I console myself with the knowledge that they were speaking from a place of ignorance and privilege, and it was never really about us.

Poor behaviour training for teachers

As I have mentioned several times previously in this book, I think teachers are superheroes. The work they do is grossly undervalued and underpaid. Nothing I say in this book is a slight on teachers personally. That said, most teacher training is woefully lacking when it comes to behaviour management, understanding child psychology and special-education needs and disabilities, especially when it comes to secondary or high-school teachers. As I mentioned earlier, my oldest son is a teacher. He took his postgraduate certificate of education (PGCE) training at an Oxbridge college, and I was shocked at how outdated and lacking the information given to him surrounding behaviour and ADHD was. If this is one of the world's 'best' universities, then what are others teaching? If our teachers arrive in classrooms with knowledge gaps and old-fashioned ideas of behaviour management, it's no wonder that so many children and their parents struggle. Again, this is not an attack on teachers – they themselves deserve better, too.

What happens when professionals – like teachers – aren't kept up to date with current scientific knowledge and training? They fill the gaps with what the media, social media and wider society tell them. And what comprises most of these messages? You've guessed it: that parents these days are too focused on being their child's friend than on disciplining them. This parent blaming adds to the 'it's-my-fault' thoughts that you are likely so accustomed to.

In the year before Flynn received an ADHD diagnosis, I was summoned to his school lots. I had meeting after meeting with his form tutor, head of year, school SENCo and deputy head. I know each of them thought I was the problem. Not because I'm paranoid, but because they told me so to my face. In our last meeting before Flynn's diagnosis a member of the leadership team told me, 'We know you have written a book called "Gentle Discipline" and we think this is the problem. You need tough discipline.' They basically called me a useless, permissive parent. It didn't matter how many research studies I quoted, how much science I discussed or how many times I tried to explain that they had clearly not *read* my book because they had completely the wrong end of the stick – they insisted my lack of discipline had caused my son's behaviour problems.

The worst part of this story is that I began to believe them. I had a huge crisis of confidence. I had sold hundreds of thousands of books, but what if I was wrong? What if I *had* caused this? Maybe everything I had stood for professionally was the problem. Maybe I was actually the problem? Slowly, after Flynn's diagnosis, my confidence began to rebuild and that doubt was replaced with anger. That anger is one of the reasons why it has taken me so long to write this book. I'm finally in a place where I think I can direct it productively and use it, hopefully, to help other parents from experiencing those same feelings of self-doubt.

The desire for quick fixes

It seems that everything in our world is increasingly geared to fast results and quick fixes. From fast food to same-day grocery deliveries, next-day loans to two-week diet plans promising dramatic weight loss, we are sucked into believing that change can be fast if only we pay enough, work hard enough or follow the right plans. One of the common criticisms I see of gentle parenting is that it doesn't work, because despite all the effort put in by parents, their toddler still tantrums, their baby still wakes at night, their tween still answers back and their teenager still won't do their homework. The thing is, gentle parenting techniques are not meant to produce short-term compliance, but long-term effects on individuals as they grow into adulthood. You can't measure the impact of nurturing, understanding and respectful parenting in hours, days, weeks or even months. The true results are seen over years, in line with the development of the child's brain. Now this idea is frustrating enough to parents of neurotypical children, but when your child is explosive, it can feel even harder to keep the faith. The answer I always give to parents is to 'find the glimmers' – look for those small moments of hope, the tiny rays of sunshine that last for a split second, rather than searching for radical change.

As parents, we have a tendency to think it is our role to make everything better for our children, and if we can't do that, we can often feel that we have failed in our role. The sad reality is, though, that we can't make everything better for them, especially not those facing discrimination and poor treatment because of their behaviour. Once again, we tend to internalise these perceived failures and blame ourselves.

The curse of comparison

From the moment our children are born, they are compared to others. How much did they weigh? How long are they? When did they first smile? When did they first sleep through the night? How many words can they say? And with each comparison, parents, particularly mothers, feel a sense of pride or anxiety. Is my baby big enough? Are they too big? Can my toddler say enough words? Are they too late to recognise their numbers? Here again, mothers tend to internalise these developmental milestones as a reflection of their parenting ability, something fathers are far less likely to do. What happens when our children are late to do something? Or they behave in a way that is different from the norm? We begin to blame ourselves, however misplaced that blame may be.

Many parents mistakenly believe that others feel better than them, that they are somehow coping better with parenting. Their children are more obedient, more polite and less explosive. The trouble is we view life through the filter of our own thoughts and feelings without realising that we are only seeing the carefully curated public image of others. While we see the front of their museum-worthy hand-embroidered piece of art, we intimately know the messy, knotted backside of our own tapestry. We are not comparing like with like.

The lack of a village

There is no doubt that we are parenting increasingly in isolation today. Gone are the days when we would raise children surrounded by our siblings, parents, grandparents, aunts, uncles and cousins. The days when the physical and mental load of child rearing was shared. Today, most families are scattered geographically, and everybody is busy with their own lives, work and family. The pressure this places on new parents in particular is immense. The internet has provided a partial village replacement, but it also brings with it a huge amount of comparison and a dark side, too. Parent-and-baby or -child groups also play a role, but for those with a child with ADHD or explosive behaviour, they can leave you feeling far, far worse. If you've been to a group and your child has had a meltdown, or acted out, you'll know how terrible it feels to be 'that parent' and 'that child', and the chances are you've felt reluctant to return.

Being a parent today is lonely work, and being the parent of a child with explosive behaviour is the loneliest place to be of all. The emotional difficulty of finding yourself in a village of neurotypical parents with neurotypical 'well-behaved' children can make you even more lonely, although you're surrounded by other parents, and the ostracisation quickly leaves you feeling that it's your fault – there must be something wrong with you. But of course there isn't – you just haven't been lucky enough to find the parents who are honest about their struggles, rather than those who make you feel uncomfortable because they're supposedly so much better than you.

What if you *have* done things wrong?

We all have. I haven't written this book to make you feel bad or judge you. I've written it to support you and let you know that you're not the only one feeling like you do. While I've no doubt that you are a good parent, I also suspect you have done many things that could be construed as 'wrong' from a parenting perspective. I also suspect you've done things that wouldn't be considered 'gentle parenting'. All this is OK. You see, I've done plenty of things that wouldn't be considered 'good parenting' or 'gentle parenting', too.

Perhaps you've found this book because you want a different way to try with your child. Perhaps you've tried all the punishments and the yelling, the reward charts and the bribery. Or perhaps you've tried removing all boundaries and allowing your child to take all the control in your family. Maybe, as happened with me, somebody in a position of authority – say, a doctor or teacher – has told you that you are the problem and that you need to change your parenting. Or perhaps you haven't tried anything at all because everything is so overwhelming you don't know where to start.

Whatever you have or haven't done before reading this book, you must understand that you could only do your best with the information and support you had at the time. All that matters is you're here now and you're willing and ready to change (or perhaps you just want some reassurance that you are already doing the best thing for your child – that's OK, too). Maybe what you did in the past wasn't great for your child, or for you, but it wasn't the cause of their behaviour, or ADHD.

We've all done things we're not proud of as parents (me included, and I'll tell you a little about my own shameful experiences in the next chapter), but to move on, we need to drop the self-blame. What can you do if you struggle to drop it? Especially in those times when you feel hopeless and exhausted? Well, that's what the next chapter is all about.

But before we end this chapter, I just want to reinforce the idea that it's not your child's fault and it's not your fault. If there is fault anywhere, it belongs to our society and those in control of it, for creating a world for neurotypical children and then blaming parents of neurodivergent children when they don't fit in.

Let's move on now to our last chapter, which is all about how to get through the toughest days and learn to treat yourself with the same kindness that you aim to show your child (and what to do when you don't quite manage it).

Chapter Ten

Coping with parental exhaustion, guilt, shame and despair

I am not ashamed to admit that sometimes my own behaviour has been far worse than Flynn's. I think we need to be more honest about our own shortcomings and mistakes as a parent – too often, this is glossed over through a veil of shame and embarrassment. And the trouble with this is that the shame and embarrassment begin to weigh us down, accompanied by their friends, guilt and regret, so that everything becomes harder, until eventually we hit a point of despair and burnout.

I know this cycle all too well. Perhaps, for me, things were even more difficult as I am supposedly a 'parenting expert' and people expect me to have all the answers. While I'm in a much better place now, I clearly remember the painful and intrusive thoughts I felt in the earlier years and the crushing exhaustion and, eventually, the sense of numbness and detachment that accompanied my lowest moments of burnout. I also remember the shameful times when my own explosive behaviour was entirely unbefitting of anybody who made a living advising other parents.

This chapter focuses entirely on you, and how you feel, because ultimately (as I'm sure you have realised by now), that is the key to not only surviving, but thriving, through these years with your child. My aim is to let you know that your feelings and experiences are normal, given the situation you are in. I only wish I'd had somebody to tell me this a decade ago. Far too much parenting advice is geared towards what parents 'should' do, positioning them as needing to be uber calm and always regulated. This sort of advice is not only unhelpful, but is also harmful, because nobody is always calm and regulated. These messages are toxic and unobtainable.

We may not be able to change our children's behaviour, but we can change our own. Which is why, in this chapter, I start from the position of recognising and owning mistakes and, most importantly, understanding how to make things right with our children, as well as giving consideration for how we can make ourselves feel better – because (just like our children), when we feel better, we behave better.

As you read through this final chapter, please know that there is no judgement from me, but only the desire to lift you out of the depths of wherever you have found yourself recently.

Containing and co-regulating when we are full up

I'm sure you've heard the cliché about the aeroplane safety demonstration, where they advise putting on your own oxygen mask before you try to fit your child's. If you don't do this, you risk passing out with hypoxia, leaving your child to fend for themselves when they are in the most danger. The same is true of raising children with ADHD or explosive behaviour. As much as we may want to put their needs first, and every fibre of our being is driving us to fight more, challenge more and push more for equity, there will come a point when we break – maybe emotionally, maybe physically or, often, both. We have to centre our own wellbeing to be the best possible parents for our children. It's such a simple idea, isn't it? But it's one that takes years, even decades, for so many parents, especially mothers, to really grasp and action. Why mothers in particular? Because so many of us have been raised to put the needs and feelings of others before our own.

As little girls, we are taught to not be 'too loud', 'too bossy', 'too needy' and 'too sensitive'. We quickly learn to bury and mask our feelings, to put on a brave face and be who everybody else wants us to be. We learn that our parents are happier when we don't yell, whine or cry, and we learn that our teachers like us more when we are quiet in class and do what is expected of us, at the right time, with few complaints. When we have children, our patriarchal society pushes us into the sexist stereotyped role of 'the good mother'. A woman who cares for her children, her home, her partner, her extended family, her friends, her pets and, if she works outside of the home, her colleagues, her clients and basically everybody and anybody else aside from herself. I'm not saying men don't fall into this cycle – they do and there are plenty of male people pleasers – however, they are not trained into this role from birth. Fathers are congratulated for being 'an involved dad', whereas the same is simply expected of women. Spot a woman walking down the street, pushing a pram and looking at her phone, and she'll quickly be berated on social media for ignoring her child. Spot a dad doing the exact same thing and hundreds of people will fawn over him for being 'such a good dad'. It is almost always the mother the school phones when her child has misbehaved, and the woman arranging the doctors' appointments. If these women work, they are expected to juggle motherhood and their career in a way that men never do. As the saying goes: 'Women are expected to work as if they don't have any children and mother as if they don't have a job.'

Therefore women, in particular, need to learn to recognise, listen to and, most importantly, act on their own needs when they have children.

Your child needs you to be calm and they need you to be able to contain their big emotions and help with co-regulation. However, if you yourself are full to bursting, there is no space for your child and your attempts at co-regulation are going to be ineffective at best when your child senses how stressed you are. The simple and yet oh so complicated answer here is that as parents of children with ADHD and explosive behaviour, we have to make space and we have to work to calm ourselves as much as possible so that we are calm enough for co-regulation to not only be possible, but effective, too.

EXERCISE: WHAT'S IN YOUR CONTAINER?

Often, when I talk about containment, parents jump straight to what I feel is point two on the 'making-space-and-being-calmer' rule list, in that they want to know what they can do to be calmer. They are eager to hear about any special techniques and tricks I can teach them – maybe some positive affirmations or breathing techniques. The problem here is that they are bypassing point one, which is understanding what they're full up with. Jumping straight into point two means that anything they do is going to be temporarily palliating a hidden issue, not resolving it. I like to use this simple exercise to help.

To find out what you're 'full up' with, take some time to think about anything that is taking up space in your head and ask yourself what you are worried about. What is on your to-do list? What are you planning? Who are you taking care of?

What is using up your physical energy? Take a pen and note these all down in the container below.

When you have finished, take some time to ponder what you are carrying with you on a daily basis. How much space do you have available to contain your child's emotions and needs? How much space do you have available to contain your own emotions and needs? Is there anything you can remove, or can you share the load with somebody else? Are there any responsibilities that you can step away from? Or can you think of any way to lessen the load a little? I know many would recommend focusing on some self-care at this point, however, I am not a fan. You see, this just adds something else to your already full container for you to do – something else you can potentially fail at, leaving you feeling even worse.

The healthier alternative to self-care

The key to being calmer as a parent is not adding more to your already full container, but removing things. Sometimes those things are tangible and practical (as per the previous exercise) and sometimes they are emotional. Spa days, mindfulness workshops, yoga classes, evenings out with friends and bubble baths are all wonderful, but they aren't magic. They are not going to do anything to the sense of guilt that runs through your entire being. They also won't help any people-pleasing tendencies. I have met too many parents who tell me 'I can't even do self-care properly', or, 'I think I must be the only person that self-care doesn't work for.' It's not them that is the issue, however, but the whole approach to believing that we can fix decades of masking feelings and a society failing to support families with a massage (and I say this as a huge fan of massages).

Perhaps one of the most impactful things you can remove from your container is self-judgement. Once we are kinder to ourselves everything is different. It is far healthier to focus on self-kindness and self-acceptance than self-care. How do you do this? I recommend asking yourself the following questions the next time your mind wanders into self-judgement territory:

1. Given the support, resources and headspace available to me at the time, could I really have done any better?
2. Am I placing too much pressure on myself to fix everything and be a perfect parent?
3. Do the guilt and judgement I carry genuinely help me to be the parent I want to be?

I am guessing that your answers will likely be 'No', 'Yes' and 'No' in that order. I know that you are too hard on yourself, and I know that these thoughts don't help you or your child. Now it's time for you to truly understand that, too, and to let go of the guilt, the shame and the embarrassment that you have been carrying for far too long.

I want to tell you a story now about something that happened to me about fifteen years ago; I hope it lifts your mood a little and that you can have a laugh at *my* embarrassment . . .

The one where I almost got arrested for drug dealing

Many years ago, when Flynn was at infant school, as yet undiagnosed, and I was trying on different careers to see which fit me as a mother, I worked briefly as a homeopath. As the remedies I dispensed were tiny pills, we used to put them into powdered lactose (milk sugar), known as Saccharum lactis (or sac lac for short). The sac-lac powders were wrapped in greaseproof paper and folded into small wraps, about the size of your little finger. I had hundreds of them stored in a cardboard box in a cupboard in a room I used as my office at the time.

Unbeknown to me, Flynn had sussed out where I kept them and helped himself to a couple of handfuls, which he stuffed into his jacket pockets and took into school one day, to share among his friends during breaktime. The first I knew about this was when there was a knock on my front door and I answered it to find two uniformed police officers standing on my doorstep. I instantly panicked. Was everybody OK? What had happened? They replied simply with, 'Can we come in?' Once we were all seated and they reassured me that my family was safe, one of them pulled a sachet of sac lac from their pocket, contained in a plastic evidence bag. They asked me 'What is this?' I proceeded to tell them that it was lactose powder, which I dispensed my homeopathic remedies in, and reassured them that it definitely wasn't anything illegal. To which they replied, 'We know. We have drug tested it.'

Apparently, one of the midday staff at school had spotted my son dishing out the sachets of white powder to all his friends in the school playground, panicked and informed the headteacher who quickly called the police. While waiting for the police to arrive they had questioned my oldest son, who was at the same school, and asked him if he knew what it was. He had replied, 'I don't know, but Mummy works from home and people come to our house and sit in her room for a bit and then pay her money and she gives them the sachets and they leave.' You can imagine how this raised suspicions that I was dealing in class-A drugs even higher.

After a reprimand from the police officers, who told me to keep the sachets somewhere safer and out of the reach of my children, they left, as stern-faced as they had arrived. To this day, I wonder if they had a good laugh at my expense when they left. I was then called in to the school to explain myself to the headteacher and to convince her that I wasn't a drug dealer and that I would ensure Flynn did not do anything like this again.

That evening, I asked Flynn why he had taken the sachets. He looked at me with big, innocent brown eyes and said, 'Because they taste nice, Mum, and I wanted to share with my friends.' I don't know if he would have done the same had he been neuro-typical, though I suspect not. Drug-dealergate is now the source of a good laugh in my family, but the embarrassment I felt for weeks, if not months, every time I set foot on school property was immense.

Good enough is better than perfect

If you are neurodivergent yourself, you may tend towards per-fectionism (I certainly do). But the constant psychological stress of setting the bar so high for yourself and never living up to it leads only in one direction: to burnout and despair. While it is admirable that you want to be a good parent, it is not sustainable to aim to be a perfect one. You are going to make mistakes every single day, and that's OK; in fact, it's more than OK – because it's important for your children to see you mess up. It is the very best way to teach them how to rectify their own mistakes.

Can you imagine how terrifying it would be for a child to have a perfect parent? Growing up never seeing their parents yelling or saying something they didn't really mean in the heat of the moment. If that is your role model, then the chances of you never living up to it are extraordinarily high. If you are constantly failing to be perfect like your parents, your self-esteem and confidence are going to nosedive. Conversely, each time you fail as a parent, you tell your child, 'It's OK to be less than perfect.' You also teach them that it's OK to be authentic in your family, to have real feelings and to let them out in the presence of those you love and who love you enough that they welcome every little bit of you – the very core of co-regulation in relationships.

That said, what we do all need to focus on is the idea of rupture and repair: it's OK to screw up, but it isn't OK to then leave your child thinking that your explosion was their fault. Even if their behaviour was the final thing to tip you over the edge, the true cause was your container filling up with everything you were trying to juggle. Do make sure your child knows that.

Parental shame

We live in a society that's highly judgemental of parents. Which is ironic considering how unsupportive it is of them. Parents today are meant to be brilliant and cope well with very little input from the state, their community and even their wider family. If they don't cope well, be that financially, practically or emotionally, others are quick to pass judgement on them. The shame I felt from ways I behaved in public when Flynn was out of control still haunts me to this day. Or rather, should I say my behaviour as a result of the shame does.

My McDonald's moment

I can remember one particular incident as vividly as if it happened yesterday, not the decade or so ago that it actually did. We had been out for the day as a family. My four children had bickered non-stop, it had rained and we were all wet, cold, exhausted – them from a day spent climbing trees, me from the mental and physical effects of having to watch four children all in different places at the same time – and starving. Driving home, we passed a service station with a McDonald's and decided to stop and eat there. Unfortunately for us, the queue to order was immense (this was before the days of ordering from electronic boards) – cue more bickering, one of them needing the toilet, constantly changing their minds about what they wanted to order and the person in front of us ordering enough food for a football team but at the speed of a snail.

My temper was down to its very last thread when my eldest child came up to me and said, 'Muuuummm, look at Flynn.'. I turned to see him climbing on top of a charity-collection container (remember the ones in the shape of a mushroom that stood on the floor – you put a penny in them which swirled around a series of ever-decreasing circles before finally dropping down – well, it was one of those) and shaking it violently. By this point, several people were staring at him and me. I felt judged beyond belief and I completely lost it. I screamed at Flynn as if he had murdered somebody. And I couldn't stop. Once the floodgates opened, my stress just spewed out and out and out. I had completely lost control, and verbal insult after verbal insult came out of my mouth. I pulled him off and continued to yell at him. At this point, an elderly lady came over to me, pointed her finger in my face and told me to 'Stop it!' She said that I was a terrible mother and that I needed to learn to control myself. I have never felt so belittled and shamed. While she wasn't wrong, and I did stop (and apologised to my children for being angry and overreacting), the damage her comments caused was long-lasting. I was supposed to be a parenting expert, and here I was being publicly berated by a stranger in McDonald's for being the worst parent she had ever seen.

My 'McDonald's moment', as I call it now, really changed how I view other parents. I used to be quite judgemental towards those I saw 'losing it' in public. Now I realise that I am seeing a tiny snap-shot of their lives. I do not know what happened in the minutes, hours or days before and do not know what happened afterwards. What I do know is that when a parent is that dysregulated, sham-ing them is absolutely no help whatsoever. I'm not making excuses for these parents – or myself. I know how I behaved was wrong (and I suspect most parents in this situation do). It's not OK for adults to treat children like this, but what we need to understand when this happens is that we are witnessing a parent who has nothing left to give, who is at rock bottom and what they need is support, not judgement. For this reason, if I see parents struggling in public now, my response is to smile and offer them a kind word, or physical help, if necessary. Letting them know that you get it, giving a suggestion of a quick trick that worked for you, or just empathising about how hard it is to be a parent sometimes can change not only their day for the better, but their child's, too. It is support from strangers that helps, not judgement.

Burnout – and what to do when you have nothing left to give

Although physical burnout – the deep-seated exhaustion that accompanies sleepless nights and the relentless physical toil of parenting, particularly in the early months – can be highly damaging, emotional burnout can be even more so. Emotional exhaustion is a major culprit behind parents' inability to control their tempers and emotions around their children, especially those with ADHD and explosive behaviour.

If we are at rock bottom emotionally, it takes very little to trigger an explosion in us, as we spill the entire contents of our container that we have been trying so very hard to keep inside – just like I did in McDonald's. Parental burnout often causes us to be triggered by our children and their behaviour far quicker than if we were in a state of physical and emotional homeostasis. As such, it is a major obstacle to being calm. Emotional burnout is the dark side of the selflessness, self-sacrifice and devotion to their children so common among parents, particularly those raising neurodivergent children.

So what can you do to help? Well, aside from what we've covered so far in this chapter, the following can also be useful:

- **Start with accepting your limitations.** You cannot do everything and be everything. Stop trying to be superhuman. Be kind to yourself and know that you are doing your best and that is good enough.
- **Set and uphold better boundaries with others.** Learn to say 'no' (it doesn't make you rude or make people hate you, I promise!). It's time to prioritise your own wellbeing if you're feeling so wrung out you don't know how to go on. You can only do that when you put your needs as close to first as possible.
- **Reset your expectations.** Often, when you're struggling with parenting, it's because you're expecting something of your children that they just can't do. Perhaps you are comparing your neurodivergent child to a neurotypical friend, or even sibling. Whoever you are comparing them to, you are going to be disappointed, because

what you're expecting of them is not in line with
their neurological capabilities, and you will only feel
frustrated when your attempts go awry repeatedly.

- **Let go of some control.** You don't need to uphold
  every boundary you ever think of with your child and
  it's OK to be flexible with them if you need to. For
  instance, if you're feeling exhausted and you would
  normally cap screen time at an hour, it really isn't
  problematic to let it go on for an extra hour or two, if
  that time gives you some much needed rest. What can
  you do to make things a little easier for yourself (and
  your child) right now?

- **If you feel the need to shout – go out!** As you know,
  I'm a huge fan of the healing properties of nature.
  Whatever the weather, dress everyone appropriately
  and get outside. Go for a walk, jump in puddles, hit
  the local playground, or beach. Getting moving and
  getting outside helps to release endorphins and will
  help you all to be calmer, not just your child.

- **Switch off the parenting advice.** Yes, this is
  incredibly ironic coming from a parenting author, but I
  find that when parents are really struggling, they bury
  themselves in parenting advice. Out come the books,
  the videos, the discussion forums – all in a desperate
  search for solutions. But this information overload can
  be incredibly disempowering for you, and if you are
  neurodivergent yourself, you can quickly find yourself
  in 'overanalysis paralysis'. If you're really struggling,
  my best suggestion is to forget the parenting books
  and advice (including this book) for a while and watch
  a funny movie instead or read a great fiction book. It
  will all still be there when you're ready for it, but this
  is a time for soul food and something that makes your
  heart feel good.

- **Check the basics: sleep, diet and exercise.** This is a catch-22, isn't it? When we're feeling rough, we tend to neglect ourselves. Our sleep goes to pot, we feel too lethargic to exercise and we tend to reach for the sugar and processed carbs. Attempting to focus on getting these back on track a little can really help. Try to get moving (it doesn't have to be an expensive exercise class – there are plenty of freebies online), check your diet in case you are deficient in essential nutrients and have an early night when you can.
- **Find some support.** Do you have a good friend, relative, partner or someone else you can offload to? If not, try to find a local neurodivergent parenting support group, or even an online one. Having somebody to speak to who really understands what you are going through can make an enormous difference.

On the final point – the need for community – if your local area doesn't have a relevant support group, is it possible for you to create one? Perhaps just online at first, at least until you can find another parent or two to share the workload with. I speak to so many parents who are desperate to meet up with like-minded others in similar situations, but they tell me there is nothing available. Can you imagine how many parents are feeling the way you are where you live? I've learned as a parent that if something I need doesn't exist, then creating it myself is a form of self-kindness.

The power of letting go

When you were expecting your child, you probably had visions of what they would look like, who they may resemble, what their personality would be like and what your life would look like as they grew. These visions and expectations are the cause of so much heartache for not only us, but our children, too. Letting go of the idea of the child you thought you would have and the parent you thought you would be is incredibly freeing.

It isn't only the expectations of how things might have been that you need to let go of. As a parent to a child with tricky behaviour, it's highly likely that you have spent the last few years building a suit of armour around yourself. And while bearing a shield to protect yourself from the judgement, the stares, the whispering, the name-calling, the dismissing of your worries by professionals and the need to build a barrier between yourself and the authorities as a defence mechanism to keep you strong for your child may have protected you in the past, letting it go is the only way for you to heal and move on authentically. Because the shield of parenting is similar to the idea of masking: it may help you in the moment, temporarily reducing stress and allowing you to fit in a little more, but there is only so long you can continue to be inauthentic, dismissing your own needs, before you burn out and despair starts to seep through the chinks. Dropping the armour means allowing yourself to be vulnerable, to share your fears and worries with others. It means letting go of the 'hard' persona that you have nurtured so carefully to help you in your fight to get your child the treatment and services that they deserve.

Letting go – lessons from nature

I am a huge fan of shadowing nature when it comes to letting go. Nature gives us gentle hints to follow with each changing season. If we listen to them, they can be one of our greatest teachers.

Winter is a time to rest, to breathe and afford ourselves time to just 'be', ready for the year ahead as we take our cues from hibernating and dormant plants. It is not a time for new-year res-olutions and pushing ourselves to be better in every way; rather, it is for storing energy for the growth ahead. Spring is about new growth and possibilities. It is a time to revisit our beliefs and actions, to ensure they still serve and grow us. It is a time to refresh our knowledge and nourish ourselves in mind and body to enable future growth as a parent. It is about sowing seeds with our children – of time, connection and understanding – to reap in the future. Summer sees our efforts begin to come to fruition. It is for family, spending time outside, noticing the changes and growth in nature. It is a time to remember how to play and re-member the wonder in small things that we held as a child. It is a time to cherish all the glimmers and to use the warmth of the sun to give us hope that we are on the right path. Autumn is a time to let go – to recognise what is no longer serving us, to make space for new growth in the future. It is a time to take stock, to harvest the good things and store the positive memories, when things went well, to see us through harder times ahead. It is a time to learn from nature that nothing stays the same; our chil-dren are always changing, as are we. What is no longer serving you that you can work to let go of today?

As we come to the end of this chapter, I wanted to leave you with some quotes from parents who have been where you are now and have learned to let go of their guilt and shame. I hope some of them resonate with you.

'I have learned that I need to try to let go of guilt that I often feel (as well as allowing myself to grieve the parenting experi-ence I thought I would have) and remind myself of my core values and parenting principles and that I am always doing my best and that my child ultimately feels safe and loved – and that counts for so much.'

'For me it's about tuning out the opinions of others. It took me a long time to get to this point, I must say, though. I've realised that all that really matters is my little family and the fact that my boy is safe and well cared for.'

'I really struggled when my daughter was younger, especially because she didn't settle very well into school. I spent a lot of time thinking that it was my fault and if I could have been stronger and kept her at home with me, things would be better for her. But she did settle and made some good friends and is now doing very well at senior school. I look back now and want to give myself a hug and tell me that everything will be OK. It sounds a bit silly, but I sometimes imagine having a conversation with the me of ten years ago, like a big sister, and it helps me to feel better.'

'I couldn't cope without our local neurodivergent-parenting support group. The friends I have made there have pulled me through my darkest days when I thought I couldn't go on any more. It makes such a difference to be in a group full of people who get it. When I used to go to a toddler group beforehand, I would feel ostracised because of my son's behaviour. Now I know that nobody is judging us and everybody just wants to help.'

'It was a long path for me, but I realise that by beating myself up I wasn't making anything better. I would just feel even more depressed and would take it out on my child who, in turn, would behave even worse. I haven't been used to being very kind to myself, as my parents were very old school and used to shout at me a lot, so it's been hard, but it helps just giving myself that grace and realising that a bad day is just that and we always have tomorrow.'

'Love. I know it sounds cheesy, but that's what got me through. The love I have for my daughter and the love she has for me. That's all that matters.'

And so we come to the end of the chapter and, indeed, the book. I really do hope I have helped you to feel a little calmer and a little more at peace. My aim when writing has been to help you to move on from a place of blame and a desire to change your child to a position of radical acceptance: of yourself, your child and who they are. As we discussed in the previous chapter, none of this is your fault, and it's not your child's fault either.

I'd like to end this chapter with the words from Flynn quoted way back in the Introduction. I wonder if they will mean something different to you now?

> *I think you have to accept the child, rather than trying to change them. Understanding and patience is the best way to help.*

I hope that I have gone some way to help you to understand and accept your child and to have some more of the patience that you need on this journey. But just remember that nobody is perfect – and that is perfectly OK!

A short closing note

In the Introduction I mentioned that I wanted this to be a book for adults who want to help children and who are willing to make changes to their own behaviour and beliefs in order to do so. My whole aim has been to write a book that is a love letter to children with ADHD and those who struggle with their behaviour, and the adults in their life who care about them. You.

So I want to thank you – not only for trusting me enough to read my words, but also for caring so deeply. I mentioned in the last chapter that what our world needs is radical acceptance of children with ADHD and those who struggle with explosive behaviour. You are a part of a much-needed movement towards that acceptance. In your day-to-day struggles it can be hard to see the bigger picture, but your efforts are helping not just your child, but others around you, too, and perhaps some who haven't even been born into your family yet.

On your darkest days please never forget the impact you can have, or the impact your child may have on the world one day. I mentioned in Chapter Two that neurodivergent children make great entrepreneurs – the unique way in which they look at the world is a privilege to witness and sorely needed today. We need neurodivergent people who think outside the box to shape our society; they were part of its evolutionary history, and I firmly believe they are part of its future, too. Your child's tricky behaviour today may well be the grit and the drive they need to make that change in the future.

I would so dearly love for individuals with ADHD – both children and adults – to be seen in a positive light, with a focus on their strengths and gifts, more than their behaviour. Can you imagine what would happen if our society, our schools and our politicians embraced the idea of equity? If there was truly a SEND and educational reform and our children were given the understanding and support they so deserve. While we may not be able to change the whole of society for our children (not yet, anyway), we can provide them with the unconditional acceptance and support at home that they need to not only survive, but thrive, so long as we take care of ourselves, too.

I want to leave you with an idea you can use when your day seems tough and you need some uplifting and a reminder that thriving is possible, even if you're not quite there yet as a family. It's the idea of looking for the glimmers – those small specks of hope that can be seen even in the darkest moments. They can be seen in your child's eyes when they look at you with pure love when you've helped them to co-regulate. They can be seen when your child makes a stranger laugh in the local park, or they put a smile on their friend's face as they greet each other in the morning. Glimmers mean seeking out the joy and finding the best in the toughest situations.

So I want to set you one final challenge before we part ways. At the end of every day, I'd like you to make a note somewhere of a glimmer that you have seen, however tiny the spark. Focus on the joy, the hope, the love and the fun, and on the days when you, or your child, need them, open your book, or your device, and read through the list for a reminder of how wonderful you and your child are.

Sarah

Resources

Sarah's social media

- Blog: www.sarahockwell-smith.com
- Facebook: www.facebook.com/sarahockwellsmithauthor
- Instagram: www.instagram.com/sarahockwellsmith
- YouTube: www.youtube.com/c/sarahockwellsmith
- TikTok: www.tiktok.com/@sarahockwellsmith
- X: www.twitter.com/thebabyexpert

Other relevant books by Sarah

- *How to be a Calm Parent: Lose the Guilt, Control Your Anger and Tame the Stress – for More Peaceful and Enjoyable Parenting and Calmer, Happier Children Too*, 2022, Piatkus
- *Because I Said So! Why society is childist and how breaking the cycle of discrimination towards children can change the world*, 2023, Piatkus

General ADHD information and support

- ADHD UK www.adhduk.co.uk
- ADHD Foundation (Australia) www.adhdfoundation.org.au
- ADHD Foundation (UK) www.adhdfoundation.org.uk
- ADD Foundation (USA) www.add.org
- CHADD (USA) www.chadd.org

General autism information and support

- Autism Society www.autismsociety.org
- National Autistic Society (UK) www.autism.org.uk
- Autism Speaks www.autismspeaks.org
- National Autism Association www.nationalautismassociation.org

SPD information and support

- Sensory People www.sensory-people.co.uk
- Sensory Processing Disorder Resource Centre www.snapcharity.org
- STAR Institute www.sensoryhealth.org

PDA information and support

- The PDA Society UK www.pdasociety.org.uk
- PDA Parents www.pdaparents.com
- PDA North America www.pdanorthamerica.com
- PDA Matters www.pdamatters.org

Speech-and-language information and support

- Speech and Language UK www.speechandlanguage.org.uk
- American Speech-Language-Hearing Association www.asha.org
- ICAN www.icancharity.org.uk

Hypermobility information and support

- The Hypermobility Syndromes Association www.hypermobility.org
- Ehlers Danlos Support UK www.ehlers-danlos.org
- The Ehlers Danlos Society www.ehlers-danlos.com

Help to get educational support

- Independent Provider of Special Education Advice (IPSEA) www.ipsea.org.uk
- Ambitious about Autism www.ambitiousaboutautism.org.uk
- Beyond Autism www.beyondautism.org.uk
- Not Fine in School (EBSA support) www.notfineinschool.co.uk

Information about alternative education

- Education Otherwise www.educationotherwise.org
- Home Education Advisory Service (UK) www.heas.org.uk
- Home Education (UK) www.home-education.org.uk

Books about ADHD for your child

- Good, L., *Wonderfully Wired Brains* (DK Children, 2023)
- Herman, S., *A Dragon with ADHD* (DG Books Publishing, 2010)
- Snape, E., *My Amazing ADHD Brain* (Vie, 2024)
- Gutiérrez, J., *Too Much! An Overwhelming Day* (Abrams Appleseed, 2023)
- Harris, N., *My Brain is a Race Car* (independently published, 2023)
- Ali, S., *The Teenage Girl's Guide to Living with ADHD* (Jessica Kingsley Publishers, 2021)
- Lazarus, S., *The ADHD Teen Survival Guide* (Jessica Kingsley Publishers, 2024)

Books about ADHD for adults

- McCabe, J., *How to ADHD* (Souvenir Press, 2024)

- Pink, R. & Emery, R., *Dirty Laundry: Why Adults with ADHD Are so Ashamed and What We Can Do to Help* (Penguin, 2023)
- Brown, K., *It's Not a Bloody Trend: Understanding Life as an ADHD Adult* (Robinson, 2024)

References

Chapter 1

1 BMJ Best Practice (2022), 'Attention deficit hyperactivity disorder in children', *BMJ Publishing Group.*

2 Young, S., Adamo, N., Ásgeirsdóttir, B., et al. (2020), 'Females with ADHD: an expert consensus statement taking a lifespan approach providing guidance for the identification and treatment of attention-deficit/hyperactivity disorder in girls and women', *BMC Psychiatry*, August 12;20(1):404.

3 Storebø, O., Pedersen, N., Ramstad, E., et al. (2018), 'Methylphenidate for attention deficit hyperactivity disorder (ADHD) in children and adolescents – assessment of adverse events in non-randomised studies', *Cochrane Database Systematic Review*, May 9;5(5):CD012069.

4 Man, K., Couper, T., et al. (2023), 'Long-term safety of methylphenidate in children and adolescents with ADHD: 2-year outcomes of the Attention Deficit Hyperactivity Disorder Drugs Use Chronic Effects (ADDUCE) study', *Lancet Psychiatry*, volume 10, issue 5, 323–33.

5 Li, L., Zhu, N., Zhang, L., et al. (2024), 'ADHD pharmacotherapy and mortality in individuals with ADHD', *JAMA*, 2024;331(10):850–60.

6 Catalá-López, F., Hutton, B., Page, M., et al. (2022), 'Mortality in persons with autism spectrum disorder or attention-deficit/hyperactivity disorder: a systematic review and meta-analysis', *JAMA Pediatrics*, 176(4).

7 Biederman, J., Monuteaux, M., Spencer, T., et al. (2009), 'Do stimulants protect against psychiatric disorders in youth with ADHD? A 10-year follow-up study', *Pediatrics*, 124(1): 71–8.

8 Biederman, J., Wilens, T., Mick, E., et al. (1999),

'Pharmacotherapy of attention-deficit/hyperactivity disorder reduces risk for substance use disorder', *Pediatrics*, August; 104(2): e20.

9   Deavenport-Saman, A., Vanderbilt, D., Harstad, E., et al. (2022), 'Association of coexisting conditions, attention-deficit/hyperactivity disorder medication choice, and likelihood of improvement in preschool-age children: a developmental behavioral pediatrics research network study', *Journal of Child and Adolescent Psychopharmacology*, August;32(6):328–36.

10 Gnanavel, S., Sharma, P., Kaushal, P., et al. (2019), 'Attention deficit hyperactivity disorder and comorbidity: a review of literature', *World Journal of Clinical Cases*, September 6;7(17):2420–6.

11 Noordermeer, S., Luman, M., Weeda, W., et al. (2017), 'Risk factors for comorbid oppositional defiant disorder in attention-deficit/hyperactivity disorder', *European Child and Adolescent Psychiatry*, October;26(10):1155–64.

12 Czamara, D., Tiesler, C., Kohlböck, G., et al. (2013), 'Children with ADHD symptoms have a higher risk for reading, spelling and math difficulties in the GINIplus and LISAplus cohort studies', *PLoS One*, May 27;8(5):e63859.

13 Ghanizadeh, A. (2011), 'Sensory processing problems in children with ADHD, a systematic review', *Psychiatry Investigations*, June;8(2):89–94.

14 Ferrer-Torres, A., Giménez-Llort, L. (2022), 'Misophonia: a systematic review of current and future trends in this emerging clinical field', *International Journal of Environmental Research and Public Health*, June 1;19(11):6790.

15 Brang, D., Ramachandran, V. (2011), 'Survival of the synesthesia gene: why do people hear colors and taste words?' *PLOS Biology*, November;9(11):e1001205.

16 Barker, M., Beresford, B., Bland, M. (2019), 'Prevalence and incidence of anxiety and depression among children, adolescents, and young adults with life-limiting conditions: a systematic review and meta-analysis', *JAMA Pediatrics*, 173(9):835–44.

17 Busch, B., Biederman, J., Cohen, L., et al. (2002), 'Correlates of ADHD among children in pediatric and psychiatric clinics', *Psychiatric Services*, 53:1103–11.

18 Angold, A., Costello, E., Erkanli, A. (1999), 'Comorbidity', *Journal of Child Psychology and Psychiatry*, 40:57–87.

19   Deavenport-Saman, A., Vanderbilt, D., Harstad, E.
      (2022), 'Association of coexisting conditions, attention-
      deficit/hyperactivity disorder medication Choice, and
      Likelihood of Improvement in Preschool-Age Children:
      A Developmental Behavioral Pediatrics research network
      study', *Journal of Child and Adolescent Psychopharmacology,*
      August;32(6):328–36.

20   Briley, P., Ellis Jr, C. (2018), 'The coexistence of disabling
      conditions in children who stutter: evidence from the national
      health interview survey', *Journal of Speech, Language and Hearing
      Research*, 61(12), 2895–905.

21   Csecs, J., Iodice, V., Rae, C., et al. (2022), 'Joint hypermobility
      links neurodivergence to dysautonomia and pain', *Frontiers in
      Psychiatry*, February 2;12:786916.

Chapter 2

1   Ohlsson Gotby, V., Lichtenstein, P., Långström, N., et al.
      (2018), 'Childhood neurodevelopmental disorders and risk of
      coercive sexual victimization in childhood and adolescence –
      a population-based prospective twin study', *Journal of Child
      Psychology & Psychiatry*, 59, 957–65.

2   Martorell, G., Bugental, A., Blunt, D. (2006), 'Maternal
      variations in stress reactivity: implications for harsh parenting
      practices with very young children', *Journal of Family Psychology*,
      volume 20(4), 641–7.

3   Roskam, I., Aguiar, J., Akgun, E., et al. (2021), 'Parental burnout
      around the globe: a 42-country study', *Affective Science*, 2, 58–79.

4   Olfson, M., Wall, M., Wang, S., Laje, G., et al. (2023), 'Treatment
      of US children with attention-deficit/hyperactivity disorder
      in the adolescent brain cognitive development study', *JAMA
      Network Open*, April 3;6(4); and Price, A., Ford, T., Janssens, A.,
      et al. (2020), 'Regional analysis of UK primary care prescribing
      and adult service referrals for young people with attention-
      deficit hyperactivity disorder', *British Journal of Psychiatry Open*,
      January 6;6(1).

5   UNICEF, 'How many children under 18 are there in
      the UK?', accessed online 24/09/24 https://data.unicef.
      org/how-many/how-many-children-under-18-are-
      there-in-the-uk/ and National Institute for Health Care
      Excellence, 'Attention deficit hyperactivity disorder: how
      common is it?' accessed online 24/09/24 https://cks.nice.

org.uk/topics/attention-deficit-hyperactivity-disorder/
background-information/prevalence/

6 Resolution Foundation (2024), 'Growing Pressures report', accessed online 24/09/24 https://www.resolutionfoundation. org/publications/growing-pressures/

7 McKechnie, D., O'Nions, E., Dunsmuir, S., et al. (2023), 'Attention-deficit hyperactivity disorder diagnoses and prescriptions in UK primary care, 2000–2018: population-based cohort study', *British Journal of Psychiatry Open*, 2023;9(4): e121.

8 Eggertson, L., (2010), 'Lancet retracts 12-year-old article linking autism to MMR vaccines', *Canadian Medical Association Journal*, March 9;182(4): E199–200.

9 Hurley, A., Tadrous, M., Miller, E. (2010), 'Thimerosal-containing vaccines and autism: a review of recent epidemiologic studies', *Journal of Pediatric Pharmacological Therapy*, July;15(3):173–81.

10 Palmer, R., Rincon, R., Kattari, D., et al. (2024), 'Assessing chemical intolerance in parents predicts the risk of autism and ADHD in their children', *Journal of Xenobiotics*; and Dimitrov, L., Kaminski, J., Holbrook, J., et al. (2024), 'A systematic review and meta-analysis of chemical exposures and attention-deficit/hyperactivity disorder in children', *Prevention Science*, May;25(Suppl 2):225–48.

11 Moore, S., Paalanen, L., Melymuk, L., et al. (20220), 'The association between ADHD and environmental chemicals – a scoping review', *International Journal of Environmental Research and Public Health*, March 1;19(5):2849.

12 Owens J. (2005), 'The ADHD and sleep conundrum: a review', *Journal of Developmental and Behavioural Pediatrics*, 26:312–22.

13 Youssef, N., Ege, M., Angly, S., et al. (2011), 'Is obstructive sleep apnea associated with ADHD?' *Annals of Clinical Psychiatry*, August;23(3):213–24.

14 Wolraich, M. L., Lindgren, S. D., Stumbo, P. J., Stegink, L. D., Appelbaum, M. I., Kiritsy, M. C. (1994), 'Effects of diets high in sucrose or aspartame on the behavior and cognitive performance of children', *New England Journal of Medicine*, Feb 3;330(5):301–7.

15 Watson, E. J., Coates, A. M., Banks, S., Kohler, M. (2017), 'Total dietary sugar consumption does not influence sleep or behaviour in Australian children', *International Journal of Food Sciences and Nutrition*, 69(4), 503–12.

16 Benton, D., Stevens, M. (2008), 'The influence of a glucose

containing drink on the behavior of children in school',
Biological Psychology, July;78(3):242–5.

17 Goyal, M., Raichle, M. (2018), 'Glucose requirements of the
developing human brain', *Journal of Pediatric Gastroenterology
and Nutrition*, June;66(Suppl 3): S46–S49

18 Calcaterra, V., Cena, H., Rossi, V., et al. (2023), 'Ultra-processed
food, reward system and childhood obesity', *Children* (Basel),
April 29;10(5):804.

19 Kemp, A. (2008), 'Food additives and hyperactivity', *British
Medical Journal*, May 24;336(7654):1144.

20 Faraone, S., Asherson, P., Banaschewski, T., et al. (2015),
'Attention-deficit/hyperactivity disorder', *Nature Reviews Disease
Primers*, 1, 15020.

21 Young, S., Adamo, N., Ásgeirsdóttir, B., et al. (2020), 'Females
with ADHD: an expert consensus statement taking a lifespan
approach providing guidance for the identification and
treatment of attention-deficit/ hyperactivity disorder in girls
and women', *BMC Psychiatry*, August 12;20(1):404.

22 Muppalla, S., Vuppalapati, S., Reddy Pulliahgaru, A. (2023),
'Effects of excessive screen time on child development: an
updated review and strategies for management', *Cureus*, June
18;15(6): e40608.

23 Gillies, D., Leach, M. J., Perez Algorta, G. (2023),
'Polyunsaturated fatty acids (PUFA) for attention deficit
hyperactivity disorder (ADHD) in children and adolescents',
Cochrane Database Systematic Review, April 14;4(4); and Granero,
R., Pardo-Garrido, A., Carpio-Toro, I. L., et al. (2021), 'The role
of iron and zinc in the treatment of ADHD among children and
adolescents: a systematic review of randomized clinical trials',
Nutrients, November 13;13(11): 4059.

24 Swanepoel, A., et al. (2022), 'Evolutionary perspectives on
neurodevelopmental disorders', in Abed, R. and St John-
Smith, P. (eds), *Evolutionary Psychiatry: Current Perspectives
on Evolution and Mental Health*, pp. 228–43. Cambridge
University Press.

Chapter 3

1 Willcutt, E., Doyle, A., Nigg, J., et al. (2005), 'Validity of the
executive function theory of attention-deficit/hyperactivity
disorder: a meta-analytic review', *Biology and Psychiatry*, June
1;57(11):1336–46.

2   Fusar-Poli, P., Rubia, K., Rossi, G., et al. (2012), 'Striatal dopamine transporter alterations in ADHD: pathophysiology or adaptation to psychostimulants? A meta-analysis', *American Journal of Psychiatry*, 169, 264–72.

3   Volkow, N. D., Wang, G. J., Newcorn, J. H., et al. (2011), 'Motivation deficit in ADHD is associated with dysfunction of the dopamine reward pathway', *Molecular Psychiatry*, 16, 1147–54.

4   Rubia, K., Mataix-Cols, D., Radua, J., et al. (2012), 'Meta-analysis of functional magnetic resonance imaging studies of inhibition and attention in attention-deficit/hyperactivity disorder', *JAMA Psychiatry*, 70, 185.

5   Faraone, S. V., Larsson, H. (2019), 'Genetics of attention deficit hyperactivity disorder', *Molecular Psychiatry*, 24, 562–75.

6   Chen, W., Zhou, K., Sham, P., et al. (2008), 'DSM-IV combined type ADHD shows familial association with sibling trait scores: a sampling strategy for QTL linkage', *American Journal of Medical Genetics, Part B Neuropsychiatry and Genetics*;147B:1450–60.

7   Sprich, S., Biederman, J., Crawford, M. H., et al. (2000), 'Adoptive and biological families of children and adolescents with ADHD', *Journal of the American Academy of Child and Adolescent Psychiatry*, 39:1432–7.

8   Demontis, D., Walters, R. K., Martin, J., et al. (2019), 'Discovery of the first genome-wide significant risk loci for attention deficit/hyperactivity disorder', *Nature Genetics*, 51, 63–75.

9   Fontana, B. D., Reichmann, F., Tilley, C. A., et al. (2023), '*adgrl3.1*-deficient zebrafish show noradrenaline-mediated externalizing behaviors, and altered expression of externalizing disorder-candidate genes, suggesting functional targets for treatment', *Translational Psychiatry*, 13, 304.

10 Demontis, D., Walters, G. B., Athanasiadis, G., et al. (2023), 'Genome-wide analyses of ADHD identify 27 risk loci, refine the genetic architecture, and implicate several cognitive domains', *Nature Genetics*, 55(2), 198–208.

Chapter 4

1   Jellinek, M. (2010), 'Don't let ADHD crush children's self-esteem', *Clinical Psychiatry News*, May 1.

2   Furukawa, E., Alsop, B., Sowerby, P., et al. (2017), 'Evidence for increased behavioral control by punishment in children with attention-deficit hyperactivity disorder', *Journal of Child Psychology and Psychiatry*, 58: 248–57.

Chapter 5

1 Kuo, F., Taylor, A. (2004), 'A potential natural treatment for attention-deficit/hyperactivity disorder: evidence from a national study', *American Journal of Public Health*, September;94(9):1580–6.

2 Taylor, A., Kuo, F. E., Sullivan, W. (2002), 'Views of nature and self-discipline: evidence from inner-city children', *Journal of Environmental Psychology*, 22:49–63.

3 Hansen, M. M., Jones, R., Tocchini, K. (2017), 'Shinrin-yoku (forest bathing) and nature therapy: a state-of-the-art review', *International Journal of Environmental Research and Public Health*, July 28;14(8):851.

4 Hansen, M. M., Jones, R., Tocchini, K. (2017), 'Shinrin- yoku (forest bathing) and nature therapy: a state-of-the-art review', *International Journal of Environmental Research and Public Health*, July 28;14(8):851.

5 Kish, A., Newcombe, P. (2015), '"Smacking never hurt me!": identifying myths surrounding the use of corporal punishment', *Personality and Individual Differences*, volume 87, 121–9.

Chapter 6

1 NASUWT (2023), 'Behaviour in Schools', September report.

Chapter 7

1 Brevik, E., Lundervold, A., Halmøy, A., et al. (2017), 'Prevalence and clinical correlates of insomnia in adults with attention-deficit hyperactivity disorder', *Acta Psychiatrica Scandinavica*, August;136(2):220–7.

2 Sung, V., Hiscock, H., Sciberras, E., et al. (2008), 'Sleep problems in children with attention-deficit/hyperactivity disorder: prevalence and the effect on the child and family', *Archives of Pediatric and Adolescent Medicine*, 162(4):336–42.

3 Cortese, S., Faraone, E., Konofal, M., et al. (2009), 'Sleep in children with attention-deficit/hyperactivity disorder: meta-analysis of subjective and objective studies', *Journal of American Academy of Child and Adolescent Psychiatry*, 48:894–908

4 Waldon, J., Vriend, J., Davidson, F., et al. (2018), 'Sleep and attention in children with ADHD and typically developing peers', *Journal of Attention Disorders*, August;22(10):933–41.

5 Liu, J., Ji, X., Pitt, S., et al. (2024), 'Childhood sleep: physical, cognitive, and behavioral consequences and implications', *World Journal of Pediatrics*, February;20(2):122–32.

6 Martin, C., Papadopoulos, N., Rinehart, N., et al. (2021), 'Associations between child sleep problems and maternal mental health in children with ADHD', *Behavioural Sleep Medicine*, January–February;19(1):12–25.

7 Hirshkowitz, M., Whiton, K., Albert, S., et al. (2015), 'National Sleep Foundation's sleep time duration recommendations: methodology and results summary', *Sleep Health*, March;1(1):40–3.

8 Durmuş, F., Arman, A., Ayaz, A., (2017), 'Chronotype and its relationship with sleep disorders in children with attention deficit hyperactivity disorder', *Chronobiology International*, 34(7):886–94.

9 Srifuenfung, M., Bussaratid, S., et al. (2020), 'Restless legs syndrome in children and adolescents with attention-deficit/ hyperactivity disorder: prevalence, mimic conditions, risk factors, and association with functional impairment', *Sleep Medicine*, (73)117–24.

10 Ipsiroglu, O. S., Pandher, P. K., Hill, O., et al. (2024), 'Iron deficiency and restless sleep/wake behaviors in neurodevelopmental disorders and mental health conditions', *Nutrients*, 16(18):3064.

11 Pockett, C., Kirk, V. (2006), 'Periodic limb movements in sleep and attention deficit hyperactivity disorder: are they related?' *Paediatric Child Health*, July;11(6):355–8.

12 Hvolby, A. (2015), 'Associations of sleep disturbance with ADHD: implications for treatment', *Attention Deficit Hyperactivity Disorder*, March;7(1):1–18.

13 Montgomery, P., Burton, J., Sewell, R., et al. (2014), 'Fatty acids and sleep in UK children: subjective and pilot objective sleep results from the DOLAB study – a randomized controlled trial', *Journal of Sleep Research*, August;23(4):364–88.

14 Vázquez, J. C., Martin de la Torre, O., López Palomé, J., et al. (2022), 'Effects of caffeine consumption on attention deficit hyperactivity disorder (ADHD) treatment: a systematic review of animal studies', *Nutrients*, 14, 739.

15 Liu, H. L. V., Sun, F., Tse, C. Y. A. (2023), 'Examining the impact of physical activity on sleep quality in children with ADHD', *Journal of Attention Disorders*, August;27(10):1099–1106.

16 Checa-Ros, A., Jeréz-Calero, A., Molina-Carballo, A., et al. (2021),

'Current evidence on the role of the gut microbiome in ADHD pathophysiology and therapeutic implications', *Nutrients*, January 16;13(1):249.

17 Bendz, L. M., Scates, A. C. (2010), 'Melatonin treatment for insomnia in pediatric patients with attention-deficit/hyperactivity disorder', *Annals of Pharmacotherapy*, January;44(1):185–91; and Checa-Ros, A., Muñoz-Hoyos, A., Molina-Carballo, A., et al. (2023), 'Low doses of melatonin to improve sleep in children with ADHD: an open-label trial', *Children* (Basel), June 28;10(7):1121.

Chapter 8

1 Baron-Cohen, S., Wheelwright, S., Skinner, R., et al. (2001), 'The autism-spectrum quotient (AQ): evidence from Asperger syndrome/high-functioning autism, males and females, scientists, and mathematicians', *Journal of Autism and Developmental Disorders*, February;31(1):5–17.

2 Hull, L., Mandy, W., Lai, M. C., et al. (2019), 'Development and validation of the camouflaging autistic traits questionnaire (CAT-Q)', *Journal of Autism and Developmental Disorders*, 49, 819–33.

3 Hinshaw, S., Owens, E., Zalecki, C., et al. (2012), 'Prospective follow-up of girls with attention-deficit/hyperactivity disorder into early adulthood: continuing impairment includes elevated risk for suicide attempts and self-injury', *Journal of Consulting and Clinical Psychology*, December;80(6):1041–51.

4 Kübler-Ross, E. (1969), *On Death and Dying*, The Macmillan Company, New York.

Chapter 9

1 Napp, C., Breda, T. (2022), 'The stereotype that girls lack talent: a worldwide investigation', *Science Advance*, March 11;8(10).

2 Fernández, M. C., Arcia, E. (2004), 'Disruptive behaviors and maternal responsibility: a Complex portrait of stigma, self-blame, and other reactions', *Hispanic Journal of Behavioral Sciences*, 26(3), 356–72.

Index

Note: page numbers in **bold** refer to diagrams.

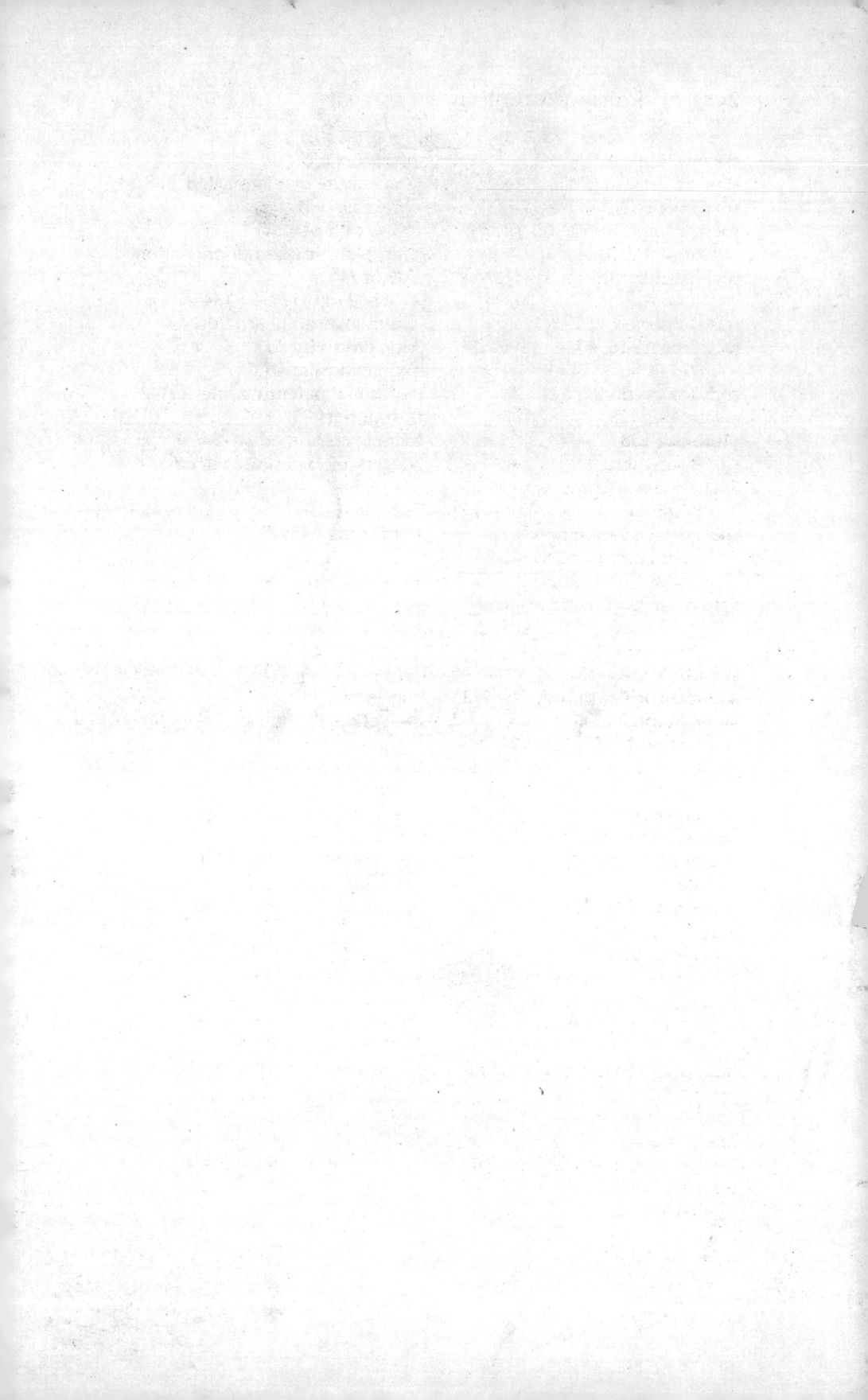